How to start a lawn care business a whole new way

A guide to creating a fun, profitable lawn care and landscape company that enriches you and others and makes the world a little better place

All rights reserved. This book may not be reproduced in whole or in part without written permission from the publisher, except by a reviewer who may quote brief passages in a review; nor may any part of this book be reproduced, stored in a retrieval system, or transmitted in any form or by any means, electronic, mechanical, photocopying, recording, or other, without written permission from the publisher

Cover art: Kenneth LaVoie

Author Photo: Deb LaVoie

Typography: Ken LaVoie

Published by Kenneth F. LaVoie – Winslow, Maine

Copyright © 2007 by Kenneth F. LaVoie III

ISBN 978-0-6151-7303-0

Table of Contents

- Intro - Listen to the beat of your own drummer

- My Story - From rags to.... GREASY RAGS!

- How I went from making $25 per hour to $60 and more per hour ALMOST OVERNIGHT!

- A Way of Being - "Everything Everything Everything shows up Everywhere Everywhere Everywhere"...

- The Plan - "Plan? We don't need no stinking plan!"

- In The Office - "Where it all begins"

    - Insurance

    - Streamline, Delegate, Batch, Eliminate

    - Clients - getting them, keeping them, knowing which ones to "fire"

    - Estimates and Budgeting - Cash Flow

- Finance, Debt and Growth - "The 50/50 Rule and stay in the black with the 20% Rule!"

- Running the Shop - Staying organized, what tools to have, getting OUT of the shop and on the road in record time!

- Equipment Lineup - Equipment and tool lineup that can increase production by 100% or more.

- In the Field - "How to be efficient, be 50%-100% faster, and use subcontractors to free up your time"

    - Mowing - Spring and Fall Cleanup - Hedge Trimming and Pruning

    - Other Services - Organic lawn treatment, chemical lawn treatment, lawn installation and more

- Sales and Marketing - "Beyond waiting for the phone to ring!"

- Principles and Philosophies - It all begins with you and within you. Take care of the inside first; the outside will take care of itself.

- Resources - Websites, books and forums to add to your knowledge base and bottom line.

- Closing – Bonus material since first publishing

Acknowledgements

As with any book, acknowledging all those who have contributed might just be impossible. So before I start, please know that if I've neglected to mention you, dear contributor and muse, it has nothing to do with your lack of contribution and everything to do with my faculties! First and foremost, my wife and daughter. My dear wife Debbie is the soul who always makes me feel just a little better than I really am. I am truly blessed and unstoppable with her by my side. My little one is my inspiration. She inspires me to do my best because I know it is a sacred obligation to teach her the same. My grandparents, Skip and Rose LaVoie for teaching me about hard work, money and what a bullshit detector looks like! My parents Ken and Dorothy for bringing me into this world and giving me the best of their unique personalities. To Troy Maddux, my "right hand man" who truly is as great a lieutenant as a man could ask for. And of course to all the contractors muses who've left their mark on my soul or at least helped me along the way with their generosity and guiding hands. Ken MacKenzie, Brandon Moore, Jeremy Mushero, Dan Misner, Adam Michaud, Keith Richards, Jesus Christ, Justin Sterling, Dennis Moreau, Stan Snow, Kevin and Keith LaVoie, Guy Mason, Kevin Fallon, Frank O'Rourke. It seems a sin to be so brief, so if I'm going to sin, I might as well sin big and stop here.

Listen to the beat of your OWN drummer.

This book is not about how to create the biggest, hottest, fastest or sexiest landscape "firm" on the planet. It's a powerful, simple "how to" for creating a profitable, simple, fun landscape "management" company that works for you and your clients, allows you to eventually "step back" and manage instead of physically work, gives you a great income with health care, retirement and tax benefits, and increases your abilities as a business person and leader in your field and your personal life as well. It's about tuning up YOUR mind and operation using simple, easy to learn systems to save time and increase profit and personal fulfillment so that you can work ON your business instead of IN it.

"WHATEVER your educational or work background, you can follow this system. I've concentrated on keeping is SIMPLE and POWERFUL. With 18 years experience, and a hunger for knowledge, I've collected enough time saving, money making tips to save you YEARS of trial and error"

I like presenting my picture of "working until noon, never working weekends, etc., but I should warn you that if you seriously put your nose to the grindstone and work 40 hours or so, with a competent helper doing the same, you can beat my numbers hands down!

I will show you:

- One tip that will save you thousands in worker's comp insurance!
- 10 rules that will cut your office time in HALF!
- What equipment to buy and what NOT to buy - specific brands and models!
- Little known resources to get equipment parts as much as 50% off the dealer's price!
- How to USE your equipment to work 50%-100% faster
- How to grow your business up to 100% or MORE without hiring ANY more employees or buying any expensive equipment that depreciates faster than you can pay it off.

The ONE service to NEVER offer to a brand new client

I'm doing it, so can YOU

My name is Ken LaVoie. I'm 42 years old, and I live in Winslow, Maine with my family. I play guitar, run my lawn care business, own a web design business and generally live life like the rest of you. I have been working on the material in this book for about as long as I've been in business and it does my heart good to share it with you now. I hope you get as much from it as I did writing it.

My lawn care business operation is a 2 man operation with

several sub contractors in place. We make $60-$70 per man hour, which is double what most contractors in our area make. We take in approx. $150,000 per year, which may not sound like a king's ransom until you realize that I only work until noon 4 or 5 days per week, haven't worked a weekend in 5 years and we live and work in Maine, where we have the shortest season of almost any state. In addition, my only employee is possibly the highest paid lawn care worker in our town, logging a little over 40 hours per week while I work, on average, less than 20. My "benefit to owner" pay is approx $47,000 per year as follows;

- My paychecks of $34,000
- SIMPLE company contribution of $1,050 (3% of total wages)
- Office and garage rent paid to us by my business of $3,600
- One vehicle (my lawn care truck) $3,000 conservative
- Partial phone and internet subsidy $600
- Health insurance deduction $1,324 (28% tax bracket x gross insurance amt.)
- Oh yeah, PROFIT!! $3-$5k per year*

TOTAL $46,574.74 - $48,574.74

I have 8 subcontractors who handle a variety of items such as mulching, hedge trimming, loaming and seeding, hydro seeding, walkways, tree installation, chipping, lawn treatments and hopefully more and more as I become more comfortable and find more competent, reasonably priced contractors. My goal at the end of 3 years is that I personally help out in the spring and fall for a few hours doing the spring and fall cleanups, then do estimates and manage the rest of the year.

From rags to .... GREASY rags!

I started my lawn care business for a great reason! It was the only way I could think of to be self employed and not go back to college!! No wonder the lawn care industry has struggled for recognition and credibility. I was making $7 per hour as a cook, and desperately wanting OUT! So I opened my doors. How hard could mowing be? I knew little about finance or business, and even less about mowing lawns but I survived. I didn't know about overhead and equipment cost so I just charged $7 per hour for myself, and $5 for an additional helper when I needed one. Phew. I'm getting depressed just writing about this.

So just when I was about to give up, Richard Parkhurst, the man who was my step father when I was a child, hired me. He and his wife Janet are still my clients today, 20 years later. I kept my day job and kept mowing a little for extra cash on the side. Then I got fired from my "day" job and I knew I had to get moving. I put an ad in the local newspaper, and in June of 1990 I was

100% self employed. I grew like gang busters, taking in information like a sponge. I consulted with a friend of mine who'd relocated to South Carolina doing the same business and he just filled me full of great tips. I was the first lawn care company in my town to own a commercial walk behind, a Velke and a Shindaiwa straight shaft commercial string trimmer. But I still wasn't charging enough.

Due to a strict visitation schedule with my little girl, I took every minute off during that visitation. If I got a visit Tuesday and Thursday, I stayed home those days - nothing else was an option. Now she lives with us and those restrictions are no longer valid, but I got used to it. I pretty much cut out at noon now unless it's the spring rush, then I slave away until 2, when she gets out of school. To be fair, I also have a web design business that supplements my income nicely now, but did not in the beginning. It all came down to "lifestyle design" and whether or not I was going to listen to the voices or my heart.

The "Big Break" that just about broke ME!

Then I got my big break. It was 1993 and I had just grossed $24,000 with myself and one part-time helper. I got my first municipal job taking care of the town's 25 acre cemetery which doubled my business. Then with that doubling came phone calls. It was like "success begat success". I went from $24,000 in 1993 to $124,000 in 1994. However, I lost money that year, spending it all on equipment and new crews "learning curve" expense. My nerves got shot, my marriage hit the dumps, I got in with the wrong crowd, got divorced, threw everything away and went bankrupt in 1996. I then started up again in 1997 after a few months of soul searching and drying out. I vowed not to make the same mistakes again, but did to some extent. My ego wanted me to have a new truck. My good sense wanted us to have newer equipment so we'd stay up and running, but my ego had spent all my good sense money. So I did still struggled but survived. Then in 2000 I met the woman of my dreams, settled down and got serious.

Take Inventory of your beliefs

Pretty much everything that shows up in your life is a direct result of those "beliefs" and "agreements" you are programmed with all your life. "no one ever got rich working 35-40 hours a week", "money doesn't grow on trees", "you've got to watch every penny", "employees will take advantage of you if you don't watch them", "you can't make money doing x, y or z", "you've got to be RIGHT THERE watching your business or all hell will break loose!". I simply decided what things were going to be like and never gave it a second thought. I didn't know what I was doing when I did that, but looking back, I realize that's exactly how it worked. Now I'm living a great life, making all the money I need, looking for ways to make more and doing my fair share of charity work and donating to my favorite causes. Our family donates 10% of it's income, roughly, to our church, daughter's school and a local hospice cause - www.hvwa.org. In addition, we volunteer uncounted hours for those causes.

Now, I get up around 4:30 am, check email, take care of any web related work I need to do, meditate, head upstairs and spend a few minutes with my family, meet my employee when he arrives around 7 and take off and do estimates and landscape work from around 730-12. Then I usually take an hour nap, do some reading, and go to work on my computer for a while, doing investment and business research, writing letters or journaling. I play with my little girl and have dinner with her and my wonderful wife, Debbie. Then around 630-7, the little one is off to bed and my Deb I have some down time watching mindless television and talking with each other. Some weekends we sit in our living room and watch movies all day, other times we spend it with extended family or traveling and yet other weekends I play guitar at a club with my country rock band "Rick West and Cherokee" www.rickwestonline.com and www.kenlavoie.com . I'm taking the whole family to Disney this year. Us and all the grandparents. It will be a blast!! And I haven't worked a weekend in 5 years.

How I went from making $25 per man-hour to $60, $70 and more per man hour almost overnight.

It was the summer of 2002 and we'd just lost our largest account, a small string of burger king restaurants that were scattered over 100 miles, the only purpose of which was to give my men something to do when times were slow. We either broke even or lost money at $25 per hour. I'd lost the accounts by announcing an increase to $30 per man hour. So suddenly I found myself with a 2 person landscaping crew with about 20 hours of work per week! Our average hourly rate for this crew was $25-$30 per hour. So I gave them each $800 bucks in cash and thanked them, apologized and set them free. That left my main "long term" employee, Troy Maddux, and myself to handle all the mowing and landscaping.

So as we began digging into the fall cleanup work later that year, we discovered something strange and wonderful. Fall cleanups that had taken 12 man hours the year before were taking us 5-7 man hours now that Troy and I were doing them. THAT'S HALF THE TIME OR EVEN LESS!! Now granted, we'd also introduced a new zero turn for vacuuming vs. our walk behind with the trac vac deck mount, but later, we discovered that EVERYTHING was taking much less time. Edging, mulching and hedge trimming were taking 20-40% less time. Almost overnight, our average hourly rate shot from $30 per man hour to $60 per man hour, topping $100 PER MAN PER HOUR on some spring and fall cleanups. Now I have to tell you, I would NEVER have had the courage to increase my rates like this, even over FIVE years, so this little occurrence was truly a gift from God.

Trusting the beat of my own drummer

This gave me one of my best lessons; Listening to the beat of my own drummer. It's so vitally important that you question every belief and ask yourself "is this the way it really has to be?" I firmly believe that 90% of what we think and believe was "put there" by our parents, peers, the books we read and the T.V. shows we watch. I am also a big believer in the law of attraction which says that your reality is a result of what you believe, NOT the other way around. I suddenly felt "free", like I had suddenly been let out of a prison. I was getting $60-$80 per man per hour simply because I wanted to and chose to. No other rationale or justification. My prices were a BIT higher than much of the newer competition but not much. We were also much more efficient, and I mean MUCH more. Troy and I had a system down so well that I swear I'd day dream through the whole day, working on "auto pilot" and be surprised when it was time to go home!

So then here we are with all this EXISTING work that we've

doubled our hourly rate on. Now we need some new work, which was the next mental and spiritual breakthrough. Suddenly I'm looking people in the eye and telling them my hourly rate when 2 weeks ago I was telling them HALF THAT amount. Scary, right outside my comfort zone. But I did it and here I am!! Now a buck a minute per man is my "mental minimum". When we earn less than that, even a buck less, I figure out why and do my best to see it never happens again. We focus on quality, quality, quality. We make enough money, so we don't have to worry about that. We make sure we deliver "knock em' dead" service and let the money take care of itself. In fact, making enough money encourages us to "repay" our wonderful clients with better and better service. It keeps that feeling of "deserving" high.

The law of attraction says that our inside dictates our outside, so it's vital we are clear that we deserve what we're making. We will only end up making what we think we deserve, no more no less.

Before you "Hang your Shingle"

There is only one time I personally recommend you do a "full fledged" business plan. When you need to borrow money that you CANNOT get anywhere else. I say this because a true business plan, though a "map" to where you're going, has much information you won't really need, use or understand. I favor

Marc Allen's' approach called the "one page plan". He also recommends a slight variation from the

www.onepagebusinessplan.com/

I suggest you read the Millionaire Course by Marc Allen to get a better feel for it, but here's the basics.

- Write down your ideal scene, set five years in the future.

- Write down your goals (extracted from ideal scene).

- Turn your goals into positive, personal, present-tense affirmations.

- Deal with doubts and fears effectively (the book provides a specific process for this).

- Write simple plans for your goals on paper.

- Take the most obvious first action right in front of you, and keep going from there.

So you basically write down your ideal scene, be brave and be outrageous. Then scan this document for "goals" that you can write down. Then write down specific tasks you can take to accomplish these goals. Remember, beginning has boldness! And hard work is simply a bunch of easy stuff that didn't get done when it should've!

Who are you? Who are your clients?

Define your market - define yourself :

Who are you as a company? Are you the guy who specializes in cemeteries and schools and other municipal properties? Or are you the one who takes care of that "select group" of wealthy, particular clients who very few have the skill and patience to serve? It's SO important to define yourself FIRST or you'll have a "mixed bag" of clients and you'll make many errors in judgment as to how to serve each type. You can be general or specific, but start defining now.

We cater to middle to upper - middle class, middle to old age, particular but not "spoiled". This is where we experience the best money, most enjoyment and greatest client satisfaction. On the corporate side, we cater to small properties who are loyal to a company who gives great service. We want companies that say "Ok, he did our property JUST the way we liked it last year, I see no reason to go anywhere else". I stay away from companies that put their properties out to bid every year. You MIGHT keep the job if you give "knock em' dead" service, but chances are, saving money will always win in the end. I Stick with small and loyal, and that just works for us.

DO occasionally take clients "above" your target, just not below. Defining yourself is another way of setting your "terms". For instance, our rate is our rate. We don't dicker. We say HOW the work gets done, the client gets to dictate the end result. I am paid on time. I do what's best for my family, I live by the golden rule and I clean up my messes and take 100% responsibility for my life. Notice there are no "or else's" at the end, no "back doors". THEN they would be called "conditions". These are NOT conditions, they are "terms". There is no room for any alternative and we do not give the alternative space to exist. Period. Most of your personal terms would be the same whether you were married, single, childless or patriarch over a brood of 11. They "define" you, and adhering to them strengthens you and compromising them weakens you.

Metaphysically speaking, when you define yourself, you invoke the great "I AM". When you firmly define yourself, you will begin to find situations drawn to you that fit your definition. You'll get calls from the "right" clients, you'll be in the "right" place for the president of the condo association to stop and talk to you, you'll happen to be the ONLY contractor that answered his phone that day when the new homeowner next door calls.

Pick two and "Know the WHY?"

Pick Two:

This is extremely important! There are 3 things you can offer; low price, great service, great quality. You can only offer TWO out of the three. What are they going to be? If it's great service and quality, don't you DARE let clients dicker with you on price. Trying to offer all 3, OR offering a "different 2" from one day to the next will do you in quicker than almost any bad business decision you can make. Who are you? It's ok to change your mind as you go along, just be clear as to why. Be clear on who you are.

I'm clear that I'm all about quality and service, which is why I hire subs and am "stepping back". All my successful business decisions can be traced back to a decision to follow these two choices. All or most of my poor decisions can be traced back to a time that I "waffled" and forgot who I was.

Know the Why!:

Know what you're going to charge and WHY. You MUST feel that there's a reason you charge $40, $60 or $80 per hour or you'll let yourself be talked out of it. Know WHY you're in business. What are your goals, what are you trying to accomplish? Where are you going? Another word for "WHY" is "purpose", and purpose gives the needed energy and passion to everything. Passion is really all you need to get going and STAY going through all sorts of conditions. Passion leads to perseverance. Perseverance leads to success. Perseverance is "heard" by God and the universe as "Hey, this is what I want and where I'm going, regardless of whatever obstacles I encounter". This is also crucial in budgeting. Know how you came up with your numbers. Do the extra work. Instead of just saying "I want to grow 20% next year", figure out what needs to happen to accomplish that. How many lawns do I need to get? Make sure you BELIEVE that you can do it, and you understand what needs to HAPPEN for you to do it and your chances will skyrocket.

Sole proprietorship, partnership, LLC or corporation?

This is one of those questions that can ONLY be answered firmly by a lawyer or tax specialist (you do have an accountant don't you?!) But I'll put my 2 cents in here.

I believe that ONCE YOU ARE MAKIING A GOOD PROFIT, an Scorp is the best way to go for the following reasons:

1. It disciplines you to keep company and personal money separate because you HAVE to pay yourself a paycheck and

CANNOT commingle funds.

2. As you make more profit, you get to dictate your paycheck and leave the rest of the profit in the company which simply gets taxed at your rate. For instance, if you are a sole proprietorship, and you make $50,000 profit you have to pay state and fed taxes PLUS social security and Medicare (self employment tax) of 15.3% (you and company side). If you are an Scorp instead, you pay yourself $30,000 and pay all those taxes on it, then JUST pay state and fed on the remaining $20,000, saving $3,060!! Setting up an Scorp is pretty straight forward. Here's a good tutorial here:

http://www.scorporationsexplained.com/scorpexplained-faq.htm

I would say that as long as your GROSS is $100,000 or less and your net before tax profit (including money you pay yourself as wages) is $30,000 or less, you should stay either a sole proprietorship OR LLC. Consult your lawyer and accountant on these matters first though.

A couple of points about incorporating:

1. DON'T buy expensive ledger and corporate package. It's only a fancy 3 ring binder and corporate seal. Google "corporate seal" if you really want one, but my

understanding is that they are no longer necessary.

2. DO spend 50-60 on an incorporating package OR a program like LLC maker because it just simplifies and clarifies everything for you. IF you are comfortable researching, go ahead, but my advice is that if you can run a business, you can incorporate yourself without a lawyer. I just bought a "maintenance package" that includes minutes and bylaws to keep everything tidy and legal.

Managing and the art of NOT managing

Ego

Ego is "that which says we are separate". It's that driving force that compels us to be better, faster, make more money and look better than the next guy. It's also that thing that's responsible for every assault, murder, war and atrocity you've ever heard or read about. For the purpose of running a business, treat your ego like a beloved pet PIT BULL. Picture yourself walking down a crowded city street with a snarling pit pull pulling you along. People get out of the way, step aside and let you through, but no one gets hurt. Let him off his leash and what happens? (Ouch!).

This is the same way with the ego. You have one, there's no denying it, but become aware of it and use it to your advantage.

When you see another landscaper in town creating a beautiful landscape, and you feel that pleasant, but urgent pang, "I KNOW I can do that!", that's EGO at it's best. It's when the terms BETTER or RIGHT AND WRONG start creeping in that you are entering the danger zone.

A big, healthy ego results in you wanting to be the best, do more, be better, learn everything you can. A big weak ego results in you criticizing the guy who came in lower than you on a bid, arguing with a client who's unhappy, refusing to take responsibility, snapping at employees who question you, and the most dangerous of all .... BUYING TOO MUCH BEAUTIFUL SEXY EQUIPMENT!! Looking good is the territory of the big, unhealthy ego.

Don't get me wrong, a good, crisp, professional image is important, it's the excess that will kill you. Use your ego. Know what it looks like, know how to keep it on its' leash. Take corrective action when you let your ego get the best of you. Get comfortable with apologizing. If you've got a big ego, healthy or otherwise, you'll probably lose control of your pit bull now and again, so pack your poo bag!

Micro Managing

For some of you, this will be the most important tip you read.

Letting go. Trusting. Being "ok" with letting your workers do things their way as long as they get the job done, on time, and meet quality standards. I had the HARDEST time with this one, and it caused me more stress than any other "quirk". You will NOT achieve excellence or much growth unless you can give up micro managing. Here's some tips and advice for moving to the next level.

1. Take at least one day off per week during the week (when work load allows) and do NOTHING but enter the work at the end of the day

2. Take at least ONE week vacation during the work season (doesn't have to be busiest, but it shouldn't be the slowest time either)

3. Make it a practice, that once trained, you tell employees the "end result" you're looking for vs. the "how". Share your vision. Let them handle the "how"

4. Tweak as you go. If your people don't perform up to expectation, don't just revert to your old ways, discover why, help them get there.

5. Ask THEM what they need from YOU on a regular basis, to do their jobs.

6. Let them know that THEIR job is to make you look good, (allow them time to crack a few jokes about what an impossible job that is!), and then let them know YOUR job is to give the whatever they need to accomplish that. It's amazing what they'll come up with.

Thinking outside the grass catcher

Allowing for the possibilities

Here's where you'll pretend that you're "reinventing the wheel". Ok, so everyone is making $25 an hour cutting a 10,000 square foot lawn, that's nice. I think I want $40. How can I make that happen? Everyone is working 60 hours per week or more, and works Saturday and Sunday until August? How can I work 4 days a week, 5-6 hours per day after June? I was lucky. Much of mine happened as a direct result of the UNCONSCIOUS use of the law of attraction. And to the "untrained eye", it would appear that a bunch of weird stuff happened and that I'm just lazy! But the formula of how I went from 60 hours a week, making $25 per hour to 17 hours per week making $60-$70 and taking home $45,000 a year is simple; I decided that's the way it was going to be, I allowed for no other possibilities nor any room for doubt or disbelief. I was going to make enough money and have enough time for my family. One thing led to another and ... VOILA!

Either OR vs. Both or Nothing

Steve Pavlina has a great article complete with pod cast on this subject here: **http://tinyurl.com/2oedkg**

He puts it so well. Basically people tend to choose "one or the other" when problem solving. OR they choose something, BUT ONLY IF another condition can happen as well. Like "I want to make $100,000 per year, but ONLY IF I don't have to work 70 hours a week". Instead, try "I am making $100,000 per year, working 30 hours per week, or nothing". The power and creative energies that will become engaged in your life will amaze you. Please, listen to this pod cast now, or at least make a note to do so in the NEAR future.

Focus on what you WANT, not what you don't want.

What you focus on grows. Period. Sure, discover and dissolve your errant beliefs, character defects, personal barriers, whatever you want to call them, but manage the percentage of time you focus and work on those. Do an 80/20 in this area too. Spend 80% of your time focusing on what you WANT, 20% focusing on "fixing" what you feel needs fixing. This 20% includes writing, praying, and reflecting on what's holding you back, getting opinions from others. It does NOT include feeling guilty, bad, or kicking yourself in the ass over and over again.

Diet isn't just for your body

In the book, Four hour work week, Tim Ferriss talks about going on a "low information diet". I concur with this opinion and I don't watch the news, I don't get the paper and I don't subscribe to many magazines. I keep violent TV and movies to a minimum and I keep a constant flow of "feel good", inspirational and educational material flowing into my mind, body and soul. Watch a "chick flick" with your wife, Cinderella with your little girl or read "The Power of Now", by Eckhart Tolle. Keep the stuff you watch and read on a "high caliber". Don't waste your precious time and life being subjected to poor quality OR the death toll in every country.

Insurance

Worker's Compensation

This insurance is a huge expense for some. One mistake thousands of lawn care contractors make is to have the incorrect classification. In the worker's comp industry, there is no classification for "lawn care", so they lump you either in landscape gardening and drivers, "park noc" or street sweepers for snow removal. Now for Maine, the landscape gardening is for installation and planting and grading, and costs around $16 per $100 in wages while the PARK NOC (Not otherwise classified) is for MOWING, trimming, hedge trimming, maintenance, spring and fall cleanup, etc. and costs around $4 per $100 in wages. Hmmmmm.. Street sweeping is for plowing and is around $7 per. This is not much of an issue as we don't log a significant number of hours doing snow. Make sure that if you do a lot of "non plowing" snow removal that you tell your agent to include THAT under PARK NOC vs. street sweepers.

I pay $800 a year for workers' comp. because I make sure I don't have ANY wages classified under landscape gardening.

If you're the owner, chances are you're not covered under worker's comp anyway, so if you do have some installation, just make sure that YOU do it and not an uncovered employee.

Auto and Liability

I don't have a lot to say about these insurances. Shop around, make sure you get BUSINESS auto. Get the equipment protection rider for your liability. This covers equipment theft and damage from something falling off your trailer, etc. If you see clients at your home, get an incidental office rider on your homeowners. Consider umbrella liability if you have a large net worth. MEET with your agent annually and know how to say no if it's clear you're being sold something you don't need.

Retirement and health

Retirement and health seem to be two things that contractors ignore due to the perceived complexity of both. Neither are particularly complicated once you eliminate all the less desirable options. Here's a rundown on health insurance, retirement plans and a few other tips:

Health insurance:

In my state (Maine), health insurance is fairly high vs. the rest of the country. I currently pay $354 for a family plan for 3 people. It has a $15,000 deductible PER PERSON with a max out of pocket of $30,000. This just means that the deductible plus any copays cannot exceed $30k for the family. This might seem frightening to some people because it APPEARS that we're exposing ourselves to $30,000 of medical liability per year, and in essence, we are, but we are clear why we buy health insurance. To simply insure against the "big stuff". We are also clear that hospitals and doctors will take payments. In fact, after a year or two of making payments, we are frequently offered "discounts" to hurry up and pay in full. We owe $4,000? Mr. LaVoie, if you pay by August 31st, you can pay $3,000 and be considered paid in full. So be honorable and pay your bills, but be clear on what you can afford and be firm. The biggest caveat: ALWAYS pay SOMETHING, and pay ON TIME or they will report you quickly to the credit bureaus, then you have to spend time on the phone straightening things out.

HSA

This is one of the greatest products ever made available to the American public, in my opinion. It is basically a savings account that is "attached" to a health insurance plan that meets certain requirements. hsainsider.org has everything you need to know about these products, but here it is in a nutshell:

1. first either get a special "HSA" type health plan OR your own health plan that meets certain requirements (high deductible, but NOT higher than certain limitations - like $5,400 individual / $10,800 family max out of pocket I believe)

2. Open your HSA

3. HSA allows you to put an amount equal to your deductible OR max of $2,400 give or take into your plan and it's tax deductible just like a regular IRA. THEN, you can TAKE IT OUT tax free for medical expenses. (even dentist, massages, medication, etc.). Now if you DON'T use it for medical expenses, you can THEN take it out for retirement and pay tax like you would on a regular IRA.

Retirement plans

To me, there is only ONE retirement plan even worth considering. The SIMPLE IRA. At the time of this writing, my understanding is that the annual fees and paperwork are too onerous to make it worthwhile for a small 1-3 person business. I invite you to research this, however, as the annual limits for a ROTH 401k or regular 401k are $15,500 per year PLUS a 6% match. With the SIMPLE, you set up an account at a bank or brokerage - I recommend Vanguard (smallbiz.vanguard.com) as they are specialists in this area and they have their act together. Here's how it works.

1. You can contribute up to $10,500 of your gross paycheck to the plan and "your company" can contribute 3% of your total wages. So if you pay yourself $35,000, you can put $10,500 of that in, and your company will put in another $900. You get $900 out of your company tax free PLUS the $11,400 each year growing toward your retirement. These amounts are a write off to both you for your contribution plus your company for it's 3% contribution. This is an amazing setup and I suggest stopping what you're doing and put "Start a SIMPLE with Vanguard tomorrow morning" on your to do list! I believe they are available to sole proprietors as well as Scorp.

The only other alternative you may want to consider is a 401K. With this plan your company can match 6% instead of 3% PLUS you can put it over $15,000 per year vs. $10,000. The paperwork and fees involved, however, are MUCH more, like $3,000 per year and above to maintain and frankly, I don't think it's worth it for the little guy. 1,000% more complication for 50% more of a deduction. Nope.

Find your "Lieutenant"

One of my biggest secrets of success is that I've found a partner who does what's best for this business. He's been with me close to 16 years and he can run the lawn care operation without me for at least several weeks. When I've had enough, he'll most likely buy me out. My clients love him, I love him and I treat him as generously as I reasonably can. I give him $15 an hour, 3 weeks paid vacation, 4 paid holidays and 2-3 bonuses throughout the year as well as a generous retirement plan. For us here in Maine, a half way decent family health insurance plan would cost over $1,000 per month per employee, so we don't offer that YET, but I do supply a SIMPLE retirement plan whereby he contributes 3% of his salary and I match him dollar for dollar. I can't over stress the importance of finding someone solid to watch your back and help you reach your goals. Without someone, you'll be doing all the work, and even with "entry level" employees, you'll spend a lot of time putting out fires and micro managing. Find a great one. Do what you need to do to keep him or her and take care of them like they're family. It will come back to you. If possible, find someone who is STRONGER in areas where you are weak for maximum synergy.

First year tip: Go it alone!

I STRONGLY suggest that for your FIRST year, you work alone. No employees, no or very few subs, no part time helpers. Here's why:

- You'll be able to concentrate on learning your trade AND learning the business end of things without the distraction of managing. Managing is an entire skill in and of itself and you'll want to make sure you have the technical side of things under control first.

- You'll be able to take your time, record how long individual tasks take you, make phone calls, etc. without worrying about another person on the payroll.

- Your first year may be frustrating. You'll make ALOT of mistakes. I'd rather have someone join me when I have a few things figured out, wouldn't you?

Take time off

I STRONGLY suggest you take time off regularly, whether it's every weekend, a 3 day weekend once a month or a week long vacation twice a year. There are certain unchangeable rules in the universe and life that make this a "good choice". Here's some food for thought!

When you step away from your daily grind, your mind quiets down a little and you begin to see the "forest" a little clearer. Bring a pad with you if you're going away on vacation. Some great ideas are bound to pop into your head! It's the "simplifying" and "stripping away" of the daily input of phone calls, time sheets, scheduling, etc. etc. that sometimes makes us myopic and narrow visioned. Getting away starts a clearing process and sort of helps us "step outside" of our business and look at it like a very well informed outsider might. You'll be pleasantly surprised at what you'll find!

Another curious thing that happens when you go away or even take a couple of days off is that at some point, you can't wait to get back and try it again! Especially if you've come up with some neat ideas or new perspectives. When I go away on vacation, I relax and enjoy myself, and in the early morning hours I jot down any thoughts or ideas I come up with. I've created entire "game plans" in less than an hour of time, simply because all the frame of reference and clutter of daily work life is temporarily removed.

So if you're the type who never takes their vacation, or you have a bit of control freak in you that can't even FATHOM leaving your business running without you, guess again. Just do it. Most of your "forward movement" in life will happen when you just say (children cover your ears) .... F*CK IT!!! And then just do it.

Work on YOU

Put at least as MUCH time into working on yourself as you do your equipment and business. I've got a very sobering thought for you that hit me like a ton of bricks around the time my Dad died 2 years ago. "You're either working on becoming the next best version of yourself ..... or you're waiting to die". It's really that simple. A couple of personal development coaches I follow recommend spending a certain percentage of your income on personal development, be it books, seminars, retreats or even psycho therapy!! (3% was the amount, if I remember correctly). I agree wholeheartedly with this. I've become a much better father, husband AND business person by following a spiritual path and chinking away bit by bit at my fears and barriers. I spend time each morning meditating, praying, and I always have a book on the law of attraction, God, business or some vein of personal development next to my chair. YOU are your very best investment. You will always fare better putting $100 on

YOUR development than in any other area. Don't forget yourself, you're worth it!

Streamline - Delegate - Eliminate - Batch

I read a book recently called the "4 hour workweek" by Timothy Ferris who talks about saving time, batching, eliminating and streamlining your time in the office. I'll talk about that too, along with specific instructions on how to run an accurate, timely office. I am not going to go into too much specific software instruction. I will add instructions ONLY if what I do is different than the typical setup, otherwise, see the software help files or website for basic instructions. There is no reason that you need to be stressed out because your paperwork is piling up or there's too much work to do. With the use of simple, effective systems, you can cut YOUR workload in half and still enjoy the same, if not more income.

Time and money saving tips:

Email

Check email NO MORE THAN twice per day. Get your clients used to that schedule. Send them all an email if need be outlining your "communication schedule".

EMAIL all estimate and invoices whenever possible. Give people a one time $5 credit or something if you need to, but GET PEOPLE USED TO receiving your bills in their inbox instead of their mail box. This saves time printing, stuffing, mailing, GETTING your money and saves money on paper, ink, envelopes and postage. I sometimes get checks on Wednesday for bills I email out Tuesday if the client lives in the same town I do.

Use, but don't abuse, the WWW

When you need advice for a specific problem, FIRST pick up the phone. ALWAYS ask yourself, "is there someone I can call that has the answer to this?" first. The internet is a tremendous source of info, but it can also eat up a lot of your time if you don't find exactly what you're looking for right away.

Office - General

Entering statement charges / invoices

I don't use invoices unless it's a corporate client that demands invoice numbers. I use the "enter statement charges" feature. Now for products and materials, the "enter statement charges" feature does NOT enter sales tax like "invoicing" does, so I create a second "current liability" account called "Other Sales Tax" or something similar and use that to post sales tax to for statement charges. You'll need an old fashioned calculator for this unfortunately. Say you sell $100 worth of mulch, you enter that as statement charge, then calculate your state sales tax rate x $100 and enter that as a charge under "Other Sales Tax" account you just created. Of course, you can do what just about everyone else in the free world does and simply use invoicing. I simply like statement charges because it's like a checkbook register. I can see every charge EVER posted for the client in one register instead of clicking on invoices to find something. Older "non business owner" clients understand statements easier than invoices as well.

Automate: If you have a mowing or other task that you perform repeatedly, enter the transaction then "memorize" it. (edit /memorize statement charge) - then set it up to remind you, say, weekly. If you don't do it, just hit "no". You can do this with ALL of your mowings and save 50% of your entering mowing statement charges.

Payroll and payroll taxes

Hire a competent accountant to handle your 941s and w-2s. I use the online system at www.eftps.com for paying the actual taxes. It's quick simple and accurate. AND if you make an error, they'll catch it MUCH quicker if you use the web vs. sending in by mail. I've gotten notices up to TWO YEARS later that I've made a $3 mistake and incurred $20 of interest and penalties as a result. USE THE WEB. Have them do your state withholding and unemployment as well.

Billing

Bill at the end of the month whenever possible to keep things simple. I cannot over estimate the value of "batching", meaning doing multiple instances of a task at one time. Email as many clients as possible. I'm actually going to start doing this for July 2007. I'm going to send bills by email for every client that has an email address, THEN, through trial and error discover which ones don't want it or cannot receive this way and make a list.

Paying bills

Do yourself a HUGE favor and signup for online banking. MOST people in the US now use online banking and it's growing daily. Here's what I do. I setup recurring bills, even bills that have a different amount each month, on automatic payment, THEN I setup the payment in quick books the same way, so my check is automatically paid online and it's recorded in quick books the same day. For items like cell phone or phone, that varies each month, I just use a "safe" amount like $100 if my bill ranges from 90- 105, I might eventually end up with a credit, but that's ok. Every few months you can skip a payment to bring it back down. Also, wait until you have 5-6 bills piled up before you pay. It's much more efficient to "batch", meaning it takes more time to pay 5 bills over 5 different days than to pay 5 bills in one sitting. I recommend paying bills ONCE per week and NO MORE.

Collecting and depositing money

Make your deposits no more than once per week (or as infrequently as cash flow allows - I sometimes have to run checks to the bank every day when cash flow is thin!). This keeps with our "batching" method of office management. Depending on your passion for eliminating wasted time, consider signing up for a check scanner. It's a little machine that you setup in your office, and instead of bringing checks to the bank, you scan them and they're credited to your account!

Computer / Software

Although a computer can eat up a lot of your time, if used properly and in a disciplined manner, can save loads of time and even get you paid faster! I use quick books PRO 2006 currently. I've tried the "contractor version" but frankly didn't use a single extra feature that the contractor version included. Last time I checked, QB PRO 2007 costs $179 - look for deals on Amazon or even eBay. DO NOT UPGRADE EVERY YEAR unless you see something really neat or special you think will change your life!! Keep it simple, upgrade every 3 years or so, or as intuit stops providing support and upgrades for the version you're using. There is a link on the resources page at the end of the book for Quick Books!

You may also wish to try out some specific lawn care /

landscape software such as "clip" http://www.clip.com/ or qXpress http://www.qxpress.com/lawn-care-software.html - I tried clip but found it "non intuitive" and the forums I subscribe to have some negative feedback with it. On the other hand, I've heard nothing but GOOD about QXpress. Frankly, I find quick books gives you just about everything you could ever need without over complicating things. Once you learn the ropes and learn how to "automate" and use "memorized" transactions, you'll think it's the simplest thing you ever used. I will provide a sample chart of accounts as well as instructions on running quick books MY way. This is NOT an end all authority on quick books, however, and you are hereby advised to join the quick books users forum at http://quickbooksusers.com/

If I had it to do over again, I'd probably grab QXpress just for the fact that it keeps tally of how many hours you've spent on each property for the year and tracks mowing time and man hour rates a bit quicker and easier than quick books.

Who makes it all possible?

Return calls

Return all calls at the end of the day during your office time, either before or after entering bills. OR make a list to bring with you and call from the road, that way you might be in the area and can stop by and visit if need be. I also have my wife call me if a client calls during the day, because I'm often working in the are the call originated from. Now instead of having to arrange a meeting days down the road, I can often meet with a client within an hour.

Surveys

Send client surveys in the "thick of it" during busy season when you're MOST likely to be falling behind or "showing your worst". You want feedback even if it hurts. I've included my sample survey, which you may adjust to fit your own needs. Add an electronic version to your website to save time and money on postage or email a copy. Also, including in the months statement saves postage as well, for those clients who still receive snail mail bills. I encourage clients to complete them by giving them a $5 credit.

Pruning Your Clients

Each year, I look keep track of jobs that might not quite fit in with "who we are". Either we cannot make the job look attractive, our personalities clash, or the price is simply too low, sometimes we even come across a client, that for whatever reason, we cannot make happy. Send these clients one of two letters. A "price increase" letter or "cancellation of service" letter. I would lean toward the cancellation of service letter UNLESS the issue is price only. By getting extra money for an undesirable client, you're sending a message to the universe and your subconscious that money is a compensation for undesirable work, in other words, you're associating "money" with "bad", and if you do that enough times, that belief will become manifest in your business and life. You'll find you suddenly have all kinds of unpleasant things to charge more money for! Do this immediately. I cannot stress the importance of keeping a "clean house". Define yourself, and keep company with ONLY those clients that help you reach your goals.

Thank your Clients

Your clients are the lifeblood of your business, and without them there would be no business. As obvious as this sounds, sometimes we forget and take our clients for granted. They can seem demanding, particular, even unpleasant if we lose our attitude of gratitude toward them. So make it a point to thank them sincerely for the work they give you, every time you see them or talk to them on the phone. It doesn't have to be anything overboard, just a heartfelt, "Hey, thanks for having us back every year like you do", or even "Thanks for the work". whatever you muster that you really "feel". Every year, send a gratitude letter. I've included several of mine as examples if you ordered the full Lawn Care Success package (www.lawnguru.net). These are very heartfelt and I work 1-2 hours on this letter each year to make sure I'm coming from the heart and giving them a unique gift. One more thing I do is take my "80-20 list" and buy nice gift baskets for the top 10-20 depending on what budget I set. I currently set this number at $500, but rarely spend it all. My wife and I go to a local shop and put these baskets together ourselves and hand deliver them. Needless to say, my clients feel appreciated!

Pray for your Clients

Nothing will keep your attitude toward your clients on track more than prayer. Praying for your clients means you're taking time out of your day and thinking and focusing on their well being. It goes hand in hand with gratitude. Set this on your schedule at least once per week.

How Much??

Estimates

I use quick books for estimating unless it's a "one time" job for a new client such as planting or reseeding, in which case I use my own template complete with job specific "fine print". In quick books, I simply adjust the current estimate for the client for the NEXT season vs. doing a whole new estimate. I add a line at top that clues me in that it's been revamped for the next year such as "Estimate for 2008 Season". If you want to keep one "pre edited" copy throughout the season, then when you print the estimate in the spring, print it as PDF (using free PDF creator http://sourceforge.net/projects/pdfcreator/) and print them all to a folder on your computer. THEN print the entire batch using your real printer for mailing to clients. I also email many of my estimates to save time, postage, paper and ink.

Budgeting

Use your QuickBooks budget religiously. Use numbers as accurately as possible. The more you work on getting these numbers "real", the more meaningful they'll be to you. I go as far as figuring out what 'percentage' of our mowing we do each month so that I can more accurately forecast my cash flow each month. I actually figure out how many "Thursdays" (paydays) there are in each month so each month's labor data at least has a "shot" of being accurate. At the end of the year, I've had some actual expenses come with $2-$3 of the "budgeted" amount. I use accrual method for estimating and profit and loss statements, but cash for accounting purposes. (much simpler). For monthly statements, you want to know what you MADE, not what you took in. But for taxes, what you "took in" and "spent" is much simpler and straightforward. Generate both a profit and loss as well as budget vs. actual each month. check where you're off more than 5% and answer the questions "why", and "do I need to do anything about it?". For me, much of the time it's simply that I plugged a purchase into the wrong month, or we had a late start due to a freak snow storm. Other times, I see that I over spent on something and I make a note NOT to spend any more in that area for the rest of the year.

Budgeting and the LAW OF ATTRACTION

Here's something you won't read in too many business books. Don't be afraid to budget HIGH for income and LOW for expenses. Be aggressive. There is great power in planning and especially putting desires and plans in writing. My experience shows that when I assume less, I get less and when I budget big, I get big. Simple as that. Don't be afraid to be wrong!! On the other hand, don't go crazy and decide you're going to double sales from $50,000 to $100,000 and put a down payment on 2 new trucks. (that violates the NEEDINESS law anyway) but "be brave" and stick your neck out JUST a little.

Out of sight, out of mind

I like to setup what I call a "sweep" account. this is an imaginary checking account that you "sweep" a set amount of money into each year and then do your best to forget about it. My advice is to go slow, and ONLY put in what you can. I made the mistake of putting a huge chunk in, then let my "real" checkbook go in the red up to the amount in my backup "sweep" account. It's worked out ok though, I used to have $3,000 in there, now I have $10,000 and I'm slowly forgetting about it!

Another "trick" is to setup a SECOND sweep account for those pesky "big" bills that come regularly, such as monthly 941 payroll payment. After payroll each week, simply sweep an amount equal to your weekly withholding into the new sweep account. Then it will be "out of sight out of mind" until 941 time. Then you have the funds on hand. The key advantage to this type of sweeping is that it keeps your checkbook "real". In other words you don't have a big GLUT of cash in there, making you think "hey, I can afford that new mower now!"

Spring Pre Pays!

I started offering my clients 10% all services if they'd pre pay for the whole year. I now have 20 clients out of 60 that send me a check every April totaling around $20,000. It's GREAT because I NEVER have to borrow money any more to get "up and running" in the spring and I can go about the business of running my business instead of checking my checkbook balance every night. 10% is a lot, but my prices are high enough that I can absorb the cost, and the price is well worth it to me personally for the "ease" of cash flow. Another option I've never tried is signing people up for "monthly" payments. Tally up the estimate for the year or season. You can either do one monthly payment for landscape stuff and one for snow, OR tally the whole year and have them pay a set amount per month for the year. The disadvantage I see for myself is that my charges RARELY stay within estimated costs. There's always a few extra mowings, maybe a few extra plants installed, etc. so I opt for "pay as you go" enhanced by my "pre pays". I put a good chunk of my pre pay in my sweep account each year, like $3,000 which permanently stays there. I'm also very cautious with all that upfront money and I actually try to service THOSE accounts first, to get some of that huge credit balance down. This is just a psychological security blanket for me.

Pre Pay Winter Expenses

I strongly suggest that you pre pay as many winter expenses as possible. Warm season is a much more predictable period, cash flow wise and you'll feel MUCH more secure going into the winter with most of your bills pre paid. I pre pay my phone, all insurances and even loan payments when money permits. It makes good organizational sense to pay summer liabilities in summer and winter in winter. Most of your bills (85% or more) will be attributable to your landscape operation, so making sure at least 85% of your bills are paid in the warm season will give you a good indicator on how your cash flow is setup. Winter will only account for 10-20 percent (if you live in NE), so make sure you're not paying more than that percentage in the winter months. Just one more way of staying organized.

Finance, Debt and Growth

"Keep your walking away costs as low as possible..."

The answer to most financial and debt related questions will vary with your temperament, financial situation and business plan. In general, I think you should have your "debt to equity ratio" be no more than 50%. Many Wall Street firms use this as a "maximum" debt level for a healthy company and you can too. To determine your DE ratio, simply add up everything you "have"(assets) and also total everything you "owe" (debt). Subtract what you owe from what you have. That's your "equity". Your equity is what's left after debt, and it's another term for "net worth". We're dealing strictly with business here though, so don't include anything "non business" in your equation. Here's the formula:

Assets Minus Liabilities = Equity

Debt (liabilities) divided by Equity = Debt to Equity (DE) ratio

An example: You have $10,000 worth of equipment and you owe $3,000 on it.

That leaves $7,000 in "equity" and $3,000 in debt. To get your actual ratio, divide the debt by the equity:

3,000 / 7,000 = 43%

That's a decent DE and you won't get in trouble with that! Your equipment will depreciate, but most likely not faster than you're paying it off.

Vow to keep your DE less than 50% and debt should NEVER be a huge worry for you. Anything more puts you in the "neediness" stage that I talk about throughout the material and invokes the "law of attraction". Does the idea of "no debt" make you feel warm and fuzzy? Then that's what you should vow. No debt whatsoever. Now many financial experts would scream bloody murder that you MUST have some debt to "leverage" your business, and if you can borrow money at 5% and earn 12% more profit ... and so on. These are all valid points, but remember,

"No financial decision in life should be made by financial criteria alone..."

ZERO interest!

Whenever possible, find a good dealer who will finance you in house. I buy most of my equipment from Teague Distributors in Fairfield, Maine and the owner, Jack Teague, finances me "in house" for no interest. As a "thank you", I don't dicker too much with him unless I know I can do MUCH better. If I need a new Z, I tell him and it's ready for me to pick up with nothing but a signature. I also pay my bill on time, every time, without exception. I also send him at least 2 new customers a year. HE IS ALWAYS GLAD TO SEE ME!

Growth! Your worst enemy or best friend?

So if you're a true male like me, you'll be salivating and grunting and fantasizing about all the "KILLS" you can make, new clients to bag, landing the new shopping center they're building and offering your stock to the public in five years on the New York Stock Exchange. Cool!! Sounds like a fun and exciting trip and a sure fire way to age quickly and die broke. Or perhaps you'll be one of the lucky ones that gets it all together and makes a mark for himself. Either way is ok. It's only business. It's only life. That being said, experts say that any growth over 20% will be financed by NEXT year's income. So if you grow 20% you can handle the additional costs associated with that growth with THIS years' profits. If you grow 30% in 2007, you're going to handle 20% of it with this year's income and the other 10% with 2008 profits. It doesn't take long to see that this formula can get you into SERIOUS trouble. Grow at a 50% clip a few years in a row and you won't see any black ink for a long time! I like to take at least 3 years at any level. I've enjoyed buying NEW equipment for US, instead of having to buy it for a new crew and make do with the old broke down equipment we're using. Growth is like a wild horse. It can be a great tool and move you across the prairie quickly, but if you don't control it, it will throw you into a bush full of "rattlers"!!

Running the shop! AND getting OUT of the shop and on the road.

Have all the tools you need to quickly do everything you need to do. Pretty simple. Have good floor jacks, a good dry place to work, a decent bench grinder or better yet, professional blade grinder (landscaperpro.com). I like a dremel for sharpening hedge trimmers. Get the one with the flexible extension. Add a decent work bench, good vise, a safe dry place to store misc. pesticides, and you've got a decent shop. That's really all I have to say about the shop. This is one of those "every man to his own preference" deals, but set it up so that it's neat, efficient, safe and buy the right tools and you've got a workable shop.

I load my trucks with EVERYTHING I will need except for special jobs. I build racks to keep our tools all organized, safe and neat. That way we're not trying to figure out what we need to pack each morning. We arrive, we say "hi" to each other, do whatever maintenance is scheduled and leave. Often times, Troy arrives at 7 a.m. and he's gone at 7:10 am. That's efficiency!! We invest in good trimmer trap racks to keep our trimmers up and out of harm's way. NEVER let equipment bounce around in the back of your truck unless it's temporary. We take one day each week to lubricate and check tires and any other little things that need our attention. Blades are sharpened almost daily and we wash our trucks, shamefully, once our busy season in July is over!! We do clean our interiors regularly though! For gas, I've purchased as many 6 gallon gas cans as our trucks will hold within reason. This has enabled us to gas up every 10-12 days vs. 4-6 days, saving around 2 hours per month in labor cost. I have one $15 per hour employee, so my "average" labor cost is pretty high!!

We outsource all our vehicle maintenance, such as tire rotation, oil changes, repairs, etc. It's just easier, quicker and we know it's done right. If you're more mechanically inclined, don't hesitate to do these things yourself but do a cost analysis. Figure out about how long it takes to do these things and figure how much you could EARN working or selling instead. We figure that whatever we do mechanically will take twice as long (conservatively) as a mechanic. It's probably more like 3 times, but even 2 times gives us the answer we're looking for. Have a mechanic do the mechanical work and we do the landscaping work!!

Most important, set everything up in a consistent, organized fashion. The less you have to think or "reinvent the wheel" the better.

EQUIPMENT LINEUP

Here is our recommended equipment lineup. Keep in mind that there are many choices of excellent and not so excellent equipment, and we've only used a small cross section of available choices. My recommendation is that if you are considering using a piece of equipment NOT on this list, run a quick search on Google like "reviews equipment-i-am-considering" or better yet, email lawn-talk@lavoieslandscape.com or the Clip Forum or even lawnsite.com for advice from other contractors. Use the leverage of OPE – Other People's Experience! Brands we use and have had overall excellent luck with:

John Deere	The best of the best
Toro	Great, though not as rugged as some.
Echo	Great for hedge trimmers, but the WORST string trimmers I've ever used
Shindaiwa	Best string trimmers by FAR I've ever used. Be careful of the new "quasi four stroke" technology, stick with 231 or 261 / 272X

Which Mowers?

If you can only have ONE mower:

If you're trying to decide on a mower and you're only going to have ONE, I'd recommend a commercial walk behind. My choice is a Toro Hydro with TBAR (NOT pistol grip). The reason I'd pick a walk behind over a Z for my "only" mower is that you'll be able to get into a lot of places a Z won't go. 45 degree slopes, tiny yards that cannot afford divots and ruts and in the spring you'll be less likely to sink due to soft ground. Now I'm talking about Maine, and we have approx. 70% of our lawns fall into the 10-20k square foot range with a few obstacles and a bank or two. If you have nothing but acreage, then pick the Z.

Riding mowers

We prefer Toro Z masters. The mid mount vs. the out-front. We've heard lots of negative feedback about the out-front "walker type" toros so stick with mid mount. We use 19HP 52" deck but if I had it to do over, I'd opt for more HP for wet spring grass. Either keep em' for 5-7 years OR trade after 18-24 months.

Wide area Walk behind mowers

When I talk about walk behind mowers, I'm referring to the BIG ones with 12-20 hp engines and 36-60 inch decks. I'll always use the term "push mower" when I'm referring to the small 21 inch walk behinds. There are a lot of great choices out there. We still have our 6 and 7 year old Toro T-bar belt drive walk behinds. We use the Z most of the time, so the added efficiency of a hydro doesn't mean a lot to us. Our next one will be a hydro Tbar though. DON'T get a hydro pistol grip. The technology is a little out of date as of this writing; you have a central lever that you push to set forward speed and the pistol grips slow you down or put the wheel in reverse. If you let go, the engine dies and the machine continues forward on it's own until the last "chug".

Oh, and if you're going to buy a commercial walk behind, don't even let it leave the shop without a VELKE or other stand on sulky attachment. I recommend the Velke in particular because it's the only one I've ever used. I was the first one in my area with one, back in 2000 and I haven't been without one since!

Trimmers and Blowers

String trimmers

We use Shindaiwa ONLY – we have a couple of T 272x which I would recommend that you have at least ONE of, but frankly, I'd also buy a 230 because it's so much lighter. Use the 272 in the spring or days when you have heavy duty trimming, use the 230 when you have lighter stuff or the weather is dry and grass is not growing fast. Trimming is the single biggest determining factor on whether or not you lose or make money mowing lawns, so be intelligent with this choice! DO NOT BUY Echo string trimmers. I don't know why, but they're just not as powerful or rugged as Shindaiwa and other Japanese brands, and they have an annoying head mounted guard that is not adjustable. (we move ours way up on the shaft so we can let extra string out which makes trimming faster).

Hand held blowers

A must have. Get a name brand like Echo or Shindaiwa. You'll use this during cleanups for hard to reach places as well as small driveways when mowing.

Backpack blowers

Don't even bother opening a lawn care business without one of these! This was the SECOND single best time saver I ever bought. (the first being the z vacuum) - you MUST get the biggest CFM and wind power here. Do NOT try to save money on "mid level" blowers. Get an Echo 755 or comparable from Shindaiwa or Stihl. You will be able to get pine needles and maple "helicopters" right out of long grass and move HUGE pile of leaves effortlessly. 90% as powerful as a big 8-11 HP walk behind blower.

Hand Tools and Other Stuff

Hand Tools

To complete your "lineup" I'd recommend an assortment of shovels. Long and short handled spades and flat shovels, DEFINITELY a "nursery" type spade for edging and cleaning up edges. Nursery spades are great for planting, digging out roots, etc. etc. etc. a MUST have before you even leave the shop. a hand digger or trowel for weeding and planting annuals, PLASTIC leaf rakes (with a supply of replacement handles - home depot), at least one garden rake, plastic or metal coal or grain shovel, broom, length of rope or chain for pulling stumps (and you if stuck!)

Other Tools

Ladders: You MUST have at least an 8' and 12' step ladder to be able to handle most of the hedge trimming jobs that come your way. I use a 12' on almost 50% of my jobs, the 8' covers the rest.

Supplies

A decent first aid kit, length of rope or chain for pulling stumps (or mowers out of mud!). Toolbox complete with recoil line, spark plugs and as many tools as you'd need to do "on the road" repairs. Jumper cables, whatever pesticides you'll need. BEE

SPRAY!! 5 gallon pails with miracle grow. (drill 10-12 holes in one side of cover and one drain hold in opposite side to make a homemade 5 gallon watering can for watering freshly planted shrubs or weekly watering of annuals)

Tractors

We don't have a tractor simply because we don't have enough work for it. If you're going to do tons of loam or you have serious DAILY use for it, by all means go for it. I simply prefer to exhaust my other options before "owning" something big and expensive.

Trucks n' Trailers

Trucks

Get 3/4 ton whenever possible. They'll just stand up to the abuse. I also recommend paying extra for the extended warrantees and selling or trading before they expire. I recommend new or nearly new if possible. One breakdown can cost hundreds of dollars in repairs as well as lost time. Especially if you're earning $60 per man hour, you DONT want to be sitting in a garage or home waiting for the mechanic to call!

Trailers

14' is the minimum I'd go here. You'll need to bring both a rider and walk behind with you (as well as rear bagging push mower) and the more room you have, the easier this will be, and your equipment will not get so banged up.

Dumping (trailer or insert)

So far we haven't purchased either of these. I tallied up the number of dumpings we'd performed and realized that the 4-6 thousand for a decent dump trailer with equipment loading capabilities was more than we needed. Don't get me wrong, we would LOVE to just touch a button and dump our load vs. spending 15-20 minutes with a pitchfork or dirt shovel, but we only dump 35 loads per year, many of them 2-4 minutes by hand, so it just doesn't make sense for us. (most of our clients have a place on their property that we can dump on). Once we have more surplus cash we'll reconsider. If you will be doing much hauling, or very few of your clients have places to dump, consider purchasing one. You will save TONS of time and energy.

Plows

We use Boss 8'2" vplow. I'd recommend either a vplow OR regular plow with wings. You'll save time even factoring in the extra time it takes to get used the extra controls for the V plow.

Vacuum systems

There are two ways you can go cleanup wise. Backpack blowers for detail work with vac equipped riding mower for big areas OR backpack and walk behind blowers coupled with a truck mounted vacuum. The latter will mean your riders will last a bit longer because you're not punishing them BUT the former, we find, is usually quicker and less susceptible to wind. You're pretty much out of commission using option 2 on a windy day, and we have at least one out of 3 windy days in the fall here. Also, with option one, you suck up leaves as you go vs. moving tons of leaves to wherever the closest location you can park your "sucker truck" is. In general, option one is more efficient. If you have enough clients to use BOTH, then do so, because option two is VERY useful and efficient in many cases and you can also make extra cash "loaning out" your sucker truck to other contractors or even offering curbside leaf removal to the neighborhood.

Hedge Trimmers and other pruning equipment

Hedge trimmers

I use Echo Hc1500. No special reason other than that's what my favorite supplier has and they've always behaved well for us. They make a more rugged Hc1600 as well, but I haven't seen it or used it. I'd always go with double sided, much more efficient. I tried top of the line electric to cut down on noise and gas and absolutely hated it. Your hedge trimming operation will go VERY SMOOTH if you also add a split shaft system complete with hedge trimmer attachment and an 8' and 12' step ladder. Also learn to use a power lift, available at most rental yards. This will come in handy for shaping large crabs and trimming maples. Check your local arborist society to see what you can and cannot do (legally) tree and height wise.

Split shaft system

The THIRD best time saving investment we ever made. I use Echo because originally they were the only manufacture that made a split shaft system that had a pole saw, broom, cultivator, edger, hedge trimmer and even string trimmer. Now if I were buying a new system, I'd probably try Shindaiwa as I have always had the hots for Shindaiwa products. I would have 2 of these as they'll get a lot of use. Have a pole pruner, hedge trimmer (or 2), edger, broom (for sand in spring). You can also do a little trick. Buy an extra pole pruner and hedge trimmer. Switch the shaft on the extra hedge trimmer with the shaft on the extra pole pruner. (the pole saw shaft is MUCH longer than hedge trimmer) - Now you'll have one short and long pole pruner and hedge trimmer. The extra length on the hedge trimmer has enabled me to save time by only having to trim one side of a tall cedar hedge, as well as enable me to do SOME jobs I wouldn't have even been able to do otherwise.

Hand Tools

I like to use the Fiskars lopper, the real short handled one that you can usually get a home depot. I also use these little cheap $6 hand pruners from Home Depot or other hardware store. they're the BEST I've ever used.

Workday, How long to work, vacations.

My setup consists of TWO One man crews. I run the landscape maintenance crew while Troy handles the mowing. We each have a trailer with our equipment, and our hand tools are kept mostly in our truck rack. Troy has the same basic mowing route each day. We create the route in the winter, make sure it's efficient then leave it alone. I do basic maintenance 2-3 times per month, adding miracle grow to my annuals, and weeding. I do any other jobs on my list and come home around 2 pm in May and then noon the rest of the year. I checkup on my subs, see how they're fairing.

I feel strongly about working a reasonable amount of hours. You don't have to come home at NOON (that's a personal choice I made that works for me based on who I am), but I strongly suggest limiting how many weekends you work and how many days you put in more than 8 hours. The world isn't going anywhere, take it easy. People "put off" family and personal time to work hard NOW so they can have all that LATER. I'm telling you it doesn't usually happen. The 12 hour days just become habit, and they become the norm. The work expands to fill the time allotted and it never really ends.

Taking time for myself and taking vacations really refreshes me and reawakens my passion for the business. Get away for at least one week a year. And as soon as possible, get away for a full week IN YOUR BUSY SEASON. That's right. Nothing trains you to "let go" and stop "micro managing" better than "yanking" yourself out of the picture. You'll get a great sense of how your worker(s) handle things while you're away and simply get used to the feeling of being "ok" away from things.

Mowing and Trimming

I have included more material here than many other services because it's a big part of our business. I've included pricing, strategy and some other tips.

I price mowing at $1 a minute per man. Very simple, very easy, very ACCURATE. This gives me $60 per man hour which is what I have decided to get for my services. Now I use a mix of methods to estimate each lawn. We work in Maine, and every yard is a little different. In fact, Id go so far as to say that there is NO typical yard or lawn! I start with a $30 minimum if we can do the whole lawn with a commercial walk-behind or z, $50 if we have to even THINK about breaking out a rear bagging push mower. From there, I take an educated guess as to how long the job will take based on "comparing" it to other lawns we have. Now if you don't HAVE any other lawns yet, this method won't help. So here's a quick bullet list of times based on size of lawn.

Follow these and you won't get in MUCH trouble and you can tweak as you go. I STRONGLY recommend that you put a clause in your agreements stating that you can increase mowing price with 30 day notice. Finishing a "one time" job that you underbid is one thing. Showing up week after week to mow a lawn for $25 that you should be getting $40 for is quite another and I don't personally believe you should be locked into that. 30 days is plenty of time for them to decide to keep you or find someone else.

1/4	acre:	Min.	$30.00
1/2	acre:	Min.	$40.00
3/4	acre:	Min.	$50.00
1	acre:	Min.	$60.00

Trimming and blowing should run approximately 50% of mowing time. So figure:

mowing time

+ PLUS

trimming, weedwacker edging and blowing (50% of mowing unless there's ditches you need to mow, fences, more than 10 trees, etc.)

+ PLUS

travel (5-10 minutes - any more and you need to question whether the account is worth doing) TIMES hourly rate equals mowing price.

There are so many variables that frankly, it's impossible to give you a clear formula. But trust yourself. A BUCK A MINUTE PER PERSON, $30 minimum period, $50 minimum if you're going to start a push mower. For HUGE lawns, you can literally measure and use this formula:

75% efficiency rating is representative of actual mowing conditions, as it allows for turns and overlapping. Formula for calculating acres per hour: % efficiency = (mph x width of cut)/99

	44-Inch Deck	**52-Inch Deck**
MPH	80%	80%
3.0	1.06	1.26
5.0	1.78	2.10
7.0	2.49	2.94

I personally think it's a good idea to do ALL your lawns at LEAST once or twice by YOURSELF so that you have an idea of how long mowing vs. trimming and blowing should take. You might record both mowing and trimming time on all or most of your lawns just once, so you have a ballpark. It's good to really be clear how long things should take so you can properly assess how your helper, if you have one, is doing time and efficiency wise, or even another crew!

Mowing Strategy

Mow first. Go up and down and back and forth NEVER around and around like you were taught when you were a kid! I go around the perimeter of property and home twice, directing clippings inward (never spray clippings on house, trees if you can help it, or beds). Then when you've got this "outline" done, pick a direction and make your lines. if clippings are visible after mowing, re mow in the SAME direction. My mowing foreman showed me this. We used to mow twice, in opposing directions, but we get better results when there's a lot of clippings if we keep our direction the same. THEN alternate direction the NEXT mowing cycle.

ONCE you're super efficient, you can weed whack first so that the long clippings get mulched up by the mower, but for the first year or two, whack last. My belief is that you'll weed whack either too much or not enough. If you mow first, it's a no brainer. You simply whack whatever's left! Slightly better appearance by whacking first though. Use trimmer to edge vertically and trim. Use blower to blow drives, walks, and any stray clippings that get into beds.

When blowing driveway, pay particular attention to the edge. Many people blow clippings TO the edge and they collect there, die and then there's visible dead grass along the edge where the drive meets the grass. Take an extra moment and blow clippings ONTO the lawn. Also, once a month, blow off the foundation - dry grass tends to collect where the siding meets the concrete foundation. PAY PARTICULAR ATTENTION TO THE ENTRANCE OF THE HOME. This is where your client enters and exits SEVERAL TIMES EVERY DAY. If you leave a mess here, they will see it 100 times before you come back again. Always take one last look at the entry, or other "frequently seen places" before leaving.

General: Size of crew

I use one man crews for mowing and maintenance, 1-2 man crews for everything else. Basically, if there's a lot of traveling and more than 4 jobs per day, use one man. Why? Efficiency. For many reasons, each time you add a man, your expenses jump anywhere from 50-70% but your income does NOT. There are now two men in the truck between jobs. So if travel is 10 minutes, there's now TWENTY man-minutes of non productive time instead of just the 10.

There's also a lot of "hidden" efficiencies to having one-man crews. There is less need for communication. Lunches seem to take less time, the crew member is more flexible and can punch out and go to an appt. or stop and get a tire repaired if need be without having to come up with a plan for the other employee. Office wise, it's easier because there's one less employee to pay, manage and / or discipline. There's one less person per crew using the equipment. Lastly, the employee of a one man crew can feel a much broader sense of "ownership". Granted, your "per man" hour costs are greater because now you have truck and trailer expenses that need to be recovered by ONE man instead of 2-3. Let's do the math.

ONE MAN CREW (per hour)

INCOME $47.50

wage $15

labor burden $4.50 (30%)

truck $6

trailer / equip $7

indirect $9 (fixed costs such as insurance, office,

etc. that do not change and are not directly related to the job)

TOTAL PER MAN HOUR $41.50

PROFIT PER MAN HOUR $ 6.00

TWO MAN CREW (per hour)

(assumes 30% reduction in efficiency, which has been my conservative experience)

$33.25 X 2 = $66.50

wage $24 (15 plus 9 for helper)

labor burden $7.20 (30%)

truck $6

trailer / equip $7

indirect*** $12 (fixed costs such as insurance, office, etc. that do not change and are not directly related to the job)

TOTAL PER MAN HOUR $56.20 / 2 = $28.11 per man hour

PROFIT PER MAN HOUR $ 10.30 / $5.15 per man hour

Now this is STRICTLY doing the black and white numbers. If you start factoring in the "off the books" stuff like the "ownership" factor, independence, one less person using the equipment, etc. you find a very desirable operation with a one man crew. All this being said, use 2 men if you want. There's nothing wrong with it and you may find it a desirable situation. Especially if it drives you crazy to work alone!!

*** *indirect per hour is $18 for whole company and assuming myself as one worker (not in the mowing picture) and my one man as another, with one man crew overhead is $9 ($9 for me and $9 for mowing man), but if we add another man, that same $18 gets divided by 3, hence $6 per man hour or $12 for a 2 man crew.*

Spring Cleanup

(see equipment lineup - Vacuum Systems for advice on alternate cleanup method)

Use a handheld and backpack blower for detail work with vac equipped riding mower (Z) for big areas equipped with a thatcher on front. DO NOT attempt spring cleanups without this attachment. It does quick work of getting up old winter debris and "waking" the lawn up. If the leaves are deep and plentiful, we go over the lawn without the thatcher engaged once, then put the thatcher down and go over again, then once more with it up to get the little stuff.

Work "with" the wind as much as possible. Get the drives and walks clean as part of your detail work. At the end you can touch them up, but if you wait till the end you'll create another mess to vacuum up. Get leaves off shrubs too. If you can, power blow areas into the woods if allowed. Our spring cleanup prices are priced at $80 per man per hour and we average 7-10 times the mowing price. Here's our system in a nutshell. You'll learn MUCH more by watching the upcoming video:

1. Park and unload - one man uses z, one back pack blower although if you see that detail work is very high (lots of gutters, sticks, paper, lots of beds with piles of leaves, etc.) then you can BOTH do detail work for a few minutes THEN separate.
2. Z starts quickly vacuuming up deeper leaves while man with back pack blower gets leaves out of beds, walks, drives and rain gutters.
3. (Z operator may take time to pickup sticks and larger debris if detail work is high)
4. Z starts going over general lawn much the same way you'd mow, with thatcher down
5. BP edges of lawn, backtrack and get leaves out of areas that Z has "back blown"
6. Z puts thatcher up and does quick "cleanup"
7. Cleanup any sand in driveway and mouth of driveway. Optional, cleanup and remove all sand from curb on property for extra touch. If you think city will take care of it that week, leave it; if not, get it now because it creates a

great impression.

8. Touch up drives, street and walks and go to the next job

Fall Prep

Simply one last weeding, yank annuals if expended, cut down perennials. We do this early to mid October. Also can give hedges and shrubs a quick haircut so that they're neat going into spring.

Fall Cleanup

Use a handheld and backpack blower for detail work with vac equipped riding mower (Z) for big areas - you will NOT need or use your thatcher for FALL cleanup. DO NOT use your thatcher in the fall as the turf is more easily torn and debris hasn't really had a chance to settle in yet, so you'll just be using up extra time for nothing. Work "with" the wind as much as possible.

Get the drives and walks clean as part of your detail work. At the end you can touch them up, but if you wait till the end you'll create another mess to vacuum up. Get leaves off shrubs too. If you can, power blow areas into the woods if allowed. Clean gutters now or in the spring. Our fall cleanup prices are the same as spring cleanup. Steps for fall cleanup are same as spring cleanup except skip sand and thatcher, add cutting down any perennials or annuals you missed with fall prep.

Hedge trimming and pruning

You'll need both handheld and shaft trimmer as well as 8 and 12 foot step ladders to be competitive here. half my accounts require the 12' ladder and pole trimmer. Do these beginning in July (in the northeast) and a quick touch up in august. Weed and fluff mulch at same time and trim any low hanging deciduous branches like maple and oak. Good time to prune dead branches on trees as well, if you're comfortable with that. Always have hand pruners in back pocket and trim out anything dead in shrubs as you're trimming. Here's a service where you'll need to have EVERYONE on the job be well versed in hedge trimming. If you're efficient, you'll take 10 minutes to cleanup each hours worth of hedge trimming. So you CANNOT have a helper with you to JUST cleanup. It just does NOT work financially.

Fertilization and lawn treatment

I now sub contract this out. It's an area of expertise in and of itself. Our gross last year was $6,000 yet there are more laws and things to worry about with this service than all our other services combined. Therefore I subbed it out. Find a local contractor if possible vs. one of the national chains. I've yet to hear much good about the "big guns" other than their marketing!! I use The Turf Doctor here in Maine. Find out their pricing, put together a program and mark it up 10-20 percent and be done with it. Use this ONLY for full service clients. I recommend subbing out to enhance only. Becoming a "broker" (taking phone calls for a service and subbing it out) is a whole other type of idea that you should learn more about before embarking on. I prefer to sub out with clients I already have a relationship with.

Organic Lawn Program

Starting in 2008 I'm going to give my clients a choice of our chem lawn treatment OR our self applicated organic program. The organic program will simply consist of corn gluten meal applied in April and either CGM or alfalfa applied in September. This is literally all a lawn EVER needs once it gets used to "non" chemical. I know a few contractors nationwide who use this program and nothing else. The CGM does have weed prevention properties if you put enough and your timing is right, BUT it is very tricky and it's best to probably alert your clients that the weed preventative control will be an added "surprise", that MIGHT happen. Use 20-30 lbs. per 1,000 square feet . twice per year. The University says weed control effective at 80 LBS per thousand, but most LCO's use 20. At 80, it will be more hideous than spreading lime!! Alert your clients that if their lawns are "used" to chemical lawn treatment, it will take 2 seasons to adjust.

Other Services

Loam and Seed / Lawn Installation

We no longer offer loaming and grass seeding of ANY KIND except for basic plow damage repair to our existing clients. 90% of our customer complaints came from this service, and it's just one of those things that's difficult to communicate to clients. i.e. watering needs, bare spots, weeds, length of time to germinate, etc. so we decided, after many fits and starts, to no longer offer it. If you MUST offer it, find a contractor who is top notch with a skid steer and can bring his own loam, follow him around. He spreads the loam, you touch it up, then call a hydro seed company and have them hydro seed. THEN setup a makeshift sprinkler system and you should be fine. Ultimately, buy some battery operated digital timers from Home Depot and make sure it all works. 20 minutes per morning and 20 minutes in evening is usually sufficient.

Mulch and Edging

Use power edger, quickly dig out with nursery spade, make sure edge is 4" deep minimum, rake out very surface stuff, use your hands to get leaves, excess mulch out from under shrubs, fluff to aerate if you have a mulch fluffer, use 10-10-10 or equivalent fertilizer on shrubs and plants, add mulch to 1" thick. Mulch doesn't need to be thick unless it's a first time mulching. Mulch decomposes and builds up over time, so just a "dress coat" is usually fine.

Regular Maintenance

Here I weed and add miracle grow (if needed) to flowers. We have a list of about 12 clients that we do this for and will make an effort to "up sell" most or all of our clients next year with this service. We simply show up, weed or spray the weeds. (you'll need a pest license for this - for Maine it's thinkfirstspraylast.org - check pesticide control or bureau in your state). Mostly I prefer to hand weed. If I keep up on it, I spend maybe 20-60 minutes max and the weeds are GONE whereas if I spray, the weeds take a week to die, then they're brown for a week before they shrivel enough to be invisible. Timing is everything. If you get there every 2 weeks, you'll be onsite 15-20 minutes, getting a lot done and earning $70 bucks an hour. If you wait too long, you'll have a long miserable job and the client will see weeds FAR too long and see charges that are a bit higher than necessary for your labor.

The ONE service to NEVER allow with a new client!:

The ONE service to NEVER introduce yourself with! If there is one service that ABSOLUTELY puts a chill up my spine, it's new lawn installation or ANY loaming and seeding. Don't get me wrong, it's not rocket science, and we've made great money doing it, BUT, 90% of our complaints come from this one service. Most of the reason is client expectations, and failing to communicate this to them. Seed often doesn't take because it has to STAY wet ALL THE TIME, not get washed away, have lots of sun, etc. So conditions have to be pretty near perfect to get good results. I've finally learned to stay away from this service UNLESS it's an established client. At least then, you have a "rapport" and you can explain things to them, and you're also on the property often enough to maybe water it for them, reseed without extra travel, etc. My advice is to ONLY offer this service to clients you've had for 3 years or more.

The DREADED One Time Mowing!:

I don't care where you live, you're going to get calls from people in July whose mower broke down in May! Or maybe their current mowing guy skipped town and left them hanging and they've been too busy to find someone else. The camp is divided on this one, and some say don't take them at all, but I DO take them under one condition. There is NO ESTIMATE!! They pay by the hour. I take a look at the lawn, if it's only a few weeks behind and the grass isn't a complete hayfield, I tell them it will PROBABLY be double the usual cost (which I also give them). Otherwise I say hourly at $60 per man per hour. I make it sound as horrible as I can. If they still want me, then it was meant to be!

Cleaning up in general

I have included a separate entry here for cleaning up messes in general, whether it's hedge trimming clippings, mulch, dirt or leaves, you can MOST impact your hourly rate by learning how to cleanup quickly and efficiently. Use a wheelbarrow for HEAVY stuff only. Don't use a wheel barrow for leaves, trimmings, etc. Use a square trash barrel, lay it on it's side and use your hand or rake to move debris into barrel. Get 90% of the pile into the barrel, rake the rest to the next pile. DONT waste time getting these piles "neat" or "just so". Quickly rake em' up, get em' in and move to the next pile. I'm working on a video to show you both the right and not so right ways!!

Annual Color (flowers)

A great little side service. I plant petunias and other annuals once a year and it adds a tremendous amount of beauty and color.

1. Use a hand trowel / pick

2. Bring wheel barrow full of good composted soil (use something from local contractor or mix up pro mix with some good loam, half and half or just use plain pro mix)

3. Bring 5 gallon pails and plenty of miracle grow

4. Optional - slow release granular fertilizer such as Osmocote

How to plant:

- make a few holes with your pick
- grab a handful of your soil
- make a depression to put plant,
- grab a six pack! (of flowers)
- dump them out, rough up the root ball or rip slightly so the roots will grow faster
- plant flower
- compress around root ball it eliminate air pockets
- after planting an area, water with MG thoroughly. This will give them a good feeding AND water out any air pockets.

NOTE: Just before leaving shop, miracle grow whatever annuals you are taking. This will give them a good head start.

Once planted, water or miracle grow 1-2 times per week for at LEAST a couple of weeks. You can continue, but once WAVE petunias get revved up, they're unstoppable and you probably won't have to do much after that.

Subcontracting Strategy:

I LOVE my newfound subcontracting strategy. When I downsized and went from $30 to $60 per man hour I was determined to stay small and streamlined for a while. Because of this, there were a lot of services that I either had to find a sub for OR turn away! I cultivated some great relationships and am cultivating more as we speak. We might be able to glean a bit more profit by doing these things in house, but we'd be TOO busy during our busy season and have thousands of dollars of unused equipment sitting around much of the year due to our ultra seasonal nature. I have a plan to outsource 95% of my landscape work by the end of next year (2008) and just keep mowing, basic maintenance, cleanups, flowers and plowing in house.

Here's a rundown:

1. Mackenzie Landscape here in town handles ALL of our mulch and loam deliveries. He charges $30 to deliver plus cost of material. I could save by purchasing by the trailer load, buying a tractor and having everything at my house. Conversely, by doing things THIS way, I have ZERO waste, he is very generous and good to us because we buy 100 yards a year from him AND we don't have to own a dump truck and trailer.
2. Sanding and salting. Same contractor handles this. The grief it saves is immense. He's cracker jack, on time, all the time and if I break down, I can send him to plow a few accounts too. Speaking of that, before getting into plowing, get to know a few local contractors and exchange cell phone numbers. Setup an arrangement where you can call on them should you get in trouble. And they can do the same to you.

Snow won't wait for you to get your truck or plow fixed,. Have a list and have it taped to your clipboard.

3. Other: I'm now attempting to sub out ALL my landscaping work and just have us do spring and fall cleanup, mowing, weekly weeding, flowers and fall pre in house. I will have this nailed by year's end!

4. Loam and seed. I don't offer this to new clients, but when I must, I batch all the jobs together, hire MacKenzie's to come with me and spread dirt, then hire a local hydro seeder to come. This really needs to be done EARLY or wait until September

5. When I do a pruning job, if I have room in my trailer, I'll load the brush and take it to my house to dump, but often, I leave it by the clients curb and make one phone call to my friend Rocky, who owns Precision Tree and Landscape, and usually that day, he picks it up for a minimum $75 charge, which is comparable to what I'd need to charge my clients for doing it myself (I charge $85 for a $10 profit per load).

Basically, with my "services" subs (one man crews that handle mulching, hedge trimming and other landscape jobs), I use a percentage or hourly rate cap. If I get $400 for a job, they get a percentage of that price. If I don't really have a firm estimate then they get a percentage of my hourly rate (with a reasonable expectation of time to complete the job). So far this has worked out GREAT. It's a win win. They have the same opportunity to make "extra" money if they bust *ss AND I will always make a profit on every job, period.

Here's another great example and one I just used this week. I have a landscape job that has a bunch of "components. First we need to cut down AND dig the roots out of all the existing shrubs, and haul the debris away. THEN, bring in planting loam, new shrubs and mulch. So I had my sub stop by yesterday and do all the easy/hard work. (Easy mentally and easy for me to explain, hard physically, hard to miscommunicate). Now everything is ready for me to deliver and plant shrubs. This is the "next level" of subbing. Taking little "pieces" of your bigger jobs, or lots of smaller ones and subbing out the aspects of those jobs that fit the model. The "model" being tasks that are time consuming, fairly simple and easy to communicate OR are outside your expertise and equipment line up.

Another example is today. Today we'll I'll be meeting one of my subs at a job where I'll be pruning trees and even felling a couple. He'll be dragging the brush into the woods. Pretty simple example, but boy it sure makes my day a lot less grueling!

Prepare for change of seasons

We take our tool racks off, exchange summer tools for winter tools and put our plows and snow tires on. I suggest making a "prep list" for change of seasons so you're not guessing. (I've included a sample of ours if you purchased my whole package vs. just the book) This is also a great time to fix anything. I've often left repairs till spring, but what happens is you forget what's really needed. Much easier and effective to take care of things now, while they're fresh on your mind. Winterize all your equipment.

Also, you can begin planning next year's marketing and equipment strategies, start creating next year's budget and this is also a good time to implement and test any new software. I like to do these things in the winter so that we can hit the ground running in April and not have too many new changes to get used to.

Snow!

We have a small snow removal route with 20 driveways, give or take. We also have 2-3 commercial locations that we plow and shovel. I recommend staying away from shoveling if you can, or at least subbing it out. We will be dropping ALL our shoveling except for one key client this winter. The benefit is that ONE person can handle the snow route vs. one plowing and one shoveling. Find someone reliable if you MUST shovel to handle this work on a timely, sub contracting basis and see how it works. OR if you have an hour or less of shoveling, you can probably absorb it and handle it yourself. You just want to keep the truck moving as much as possible. We've discovered that we can do 3 $20 driveways in the time it takes us to do ONE $30 driveway with shoveling included.

Here's how I recommend charging for snow plowing:

- $100 per man hour (or $150 to $200 per TRUCK hour)
- Price drives PER VISIT, NOT per storm - you don't know how many times you'll visit per storm
- Alternately, give them a "price per season" and base it on average number of storms in your area (I like 15) and twice per storm for total of 30 visits. I also throw a "guarantee" in that says the price is good for 12-18 storms (24-36 visits) - any LESS and the client gets a refund for the difference, any MORE and I bill for the difference. This is a great arrangement because chances are high that the winter will fall into the 12-18 storm range PLUS we're both protected financially if we have an errant winter.

Your Job / Their Job

A quick note about managing and overcoming the "hermit" syndrome. I'm not sure about women, but I know that men have a tendency to simply put their nose to the grindstone when they're working and ignore everything around them and just focus on the task at hand. If you have employees, or subs, you'll need to keep a part of your awareness on those things. Don't micromanage but keep an eye on things. Make sure people are following efficient protocol, have enough to do and have everything they need. Your subs and employees jobs are to make you and your company look good. YOUR job is to give them EVERYTHING THEY NEED to do that. That's it, in a nutshell. Pretty simple, hey?

The Science of Subs

1. Seasonal Climate

Here in Maine, we work only 6-7 months steadily and predictably and 1-2 months "part time" and then we have a solid four month winter. Now my experience has shown that most people we hire and train find alternate employment during the winter, then stay with that job, leaving us in a position to find, hire and train a new employee. Now training is probably the least profitable period for a lawn care contractor. Not only is the new employee learning, but whomever is training him or her is going to be less productive while the training is going on. This is ok, it's part of life and part of the business game, but what I like about hiring subs instead is that they're ALREADY trained, they ALREADY have a plan for winter, and they're going to be back in business next year, AND they have their own work load to keep them busy when you can't.

2. Less equipment purchase

With subs, you don't have to supply the equipment. In fact, you SHOULDN'T supply the equipment, because that's one of the criteria the IRS and other agencies use to decide whether someone is really a sub OR an employee. You pay for equipment and manpower WHEN IT'S BEING USED, not when it's sitting idle.

3. Pay for results, not time

This may be the most important. You make payment arrangements to pay the subcontractor MOSTLY by the "job". In other words, if it's a $400 hedge trimming, you pay them $250-$300, depending on your own arrangements, and you pay that amount whether it takes them ONE hour or TEN hours. This follows the golden rule of "treat others how you wish to be treated" as well as the spiritual rule of "to get something, give it away". You're holding them accountable to a certain price, AND, if they're efficient and get done quicker, you're sharing in the profits with them.

4. Less management

With subs, they are their own "managers". They manage their own time, resources and work load. You simply let them know what needs to be done, by when, and set a few standards. Other than that, they're on their own, letting you tend to bigger and better things.

5. What to use subs FOR

I like to use subs for 2 different areas; Big, time consuming, simple tasks such as mulching, edging and cleanup type work. Items that don't require highly skilled individuals, but are still part of your business and need to be done. Secondly, I like to use them for highly SPECIALIZED jobs, OR jobs where they have the required equipment and I don't. This is where I use The Turf Doctor for all my pesticide coverage and MacKenzie Landscape for all my big tree planting, mulch and loam deliveries and lawn installation. Eventually, I'm going to begin to sub out SOME of our mowing. What I look for is to clean our plate of large, time consuming tasks that can be handled just as competently by someone else so that we can focus on getting more work and taking even better care of the clients we have.

6. Agreements and Payment

If you ordered my complete package, I've included both a total sub contractor agreement (which I'll update periodically) as well as my payment formula. Basically, the payment formula is based on them getting a percentage of the job estimate, with an underlying hourly rate. See documents for more details. To upgrade to the complete package, go to **www.tinyurl.com/2qy5cb**

Resources and Publications

Do your due diligence. Make sure you're hiring real SUBS and not just paying employees as subs. You'll need to address the IRS, your state taxing agency, unemployment AND worker's comp board just to make sure. Here's a great article to read concerning this issue. **http://tinyurl.com/2v9huw**

Sales and Marketing

Ok, so I admit it, I'm a lazybones when it comes to sales and marketing. In addition, once I downsized and had my "30 to 60" event, I stopped taking new clients for a while so we could hone our operation. I got used to "not looking" and I just wait for the phone to ring. That being said, I will list some great resources for marketing and marketing education, but here's a few things I employ to keep a steady stream of work coming:

Look to existing clients first

There's an amazing amount of work you can drum up from your existing client list. They already trust you, the "ice" is already broken so they're much more likely to give you a "yes" than the guy who lives across town you cold called or sent a flyer to. Some extras that we're selling this and next year are plow damage repair (lawns), aeration, organic fertilization programs and weekly weeding. Add notes or "reminders" about the benefits of aeration or lime with their monthly statements or email all your clients and ask if there's anything extra they've been putting off.

Yellow pages

You can get a free yellow pages listing simply by having a business phone line. Many contractors claim that they get many 'price shoppers', but my experience is that it's the first place MOST people look when they need something. I live in rural Maine, so the computer is a VERY distant second for most people in this area.

Newspaper

If you're looking to get a lot of business quickly, this has been my number one source. You'll get lots of calls from all over, and all types of people, but if you want to get "up and running" stick to the classifieds, and if you want to discourage "tire kickers" add a minimum price that's pretty high, like "weekly mowing starting at $30" or something similar.

Website

A must have. More and more clients communicate with vendors through their websites. Many companies won't even do business with you without one. My web design company, Central Maine Web, can set you up with a special package JUST for Lawn Guru subscribers. Visit Central Maine Web online at www.CentralMaineWeb.com

Door Hangers

I've heard a few contractors having great luck direct mailing OR hiring a couple of young kids to hang sales flyers or door hangers door to door in certain neighborhoods. Worth a try. I've never done it, but when I do I'll update my results.

Site Signs

NEBS business forms is a great source. These are small signs you place on your job sites so that people passing by see the quality of your work. This increases your exposure because otherwise, they only know it's YOU doing the work when your TRUCK is parked there. With a sign, everyone passing by knows it's your work all day, every day for as long as you leave the sign!

Truck Lettering and T-Shirts

This is probably the most cost effective advertising you can buy, simply because it's a "one time cost". Nice shirts display your name with pride and customers associate YOUR appearance with the quality of your work. Truck lettering also works wonders for the image of your company. I've lost count of the number of times I've been at a function and someone asks "what do you do?" and I reply "I own LaVoie's Landscape Mgmt." and they say "Oh, yeah, I see your trucks EVERYWHERE". We only have 2 trucks, but the fact that they clearly announce themselves makes them stick in people's minds.

Other marketing tips and resources.

Join the local chamber of commerce. There's a unwritten rule that chamber members hire other chamber members whenever possible. Also, my chamber has a local newsletter that accepts "member news". Every time you get a new account, hire a new person, write a blurb. They're HAPPY to have something to put in the newsletter as it's mostly volunteer contributed.

Do Unto Others

Do charity work. This is something every company should do

anyway, without expectation. However, doing charity work does have added marketing benefits as it shows the community what kind of people you are. I think people are more likely to hire an outfit that they see giving back to the community. There's just something more warm and fuzzy about the local lawn care guy mowing the homeless shelter for free.

Tips for Better Business and Better Living

Some of these tips are business specific, others are tips and philosophies about a "way of being". When you adopt a way of being that is gentle, non resistant and positive, your life simply becomes .... simpler. easier, more fun, more productive. If you read NOTHING ELSE in this program, read this.

80-20 Rule

approximately 20 percent of your clients will bring in 80 of your joy. I use the term Joy here because I like to focus on the "whole" picture vs. just profits. While it's true that 20% of my clients bring in 80% of my gross income, there's a few that don't quite make the "money" list that I include on the "joy" list because they're just great clients. I put a value on clients who appreciate us, and who just let us do our jobs and do them the way we like. I'll take a few bucks less an hour for those clients.

But the truth is .. I don't have to. Most of my favorite clients are also my most profitable ones. Go figure! Use this rule in EVERYTHING EVERYTHING EVERYTHING you do. Use it especially with your time. Chances are, 80% of what you do is borderline unproductive or even unnecessary and you wouldn't even do it if you didn't think you HAD to. So KNOW who your 20% are. Make a list and keep it with you. What I do is to look at MY 20% list when I'm wondering who has to "come next" during those times I'm overwhelmed and we've fallen behind. That way I'm using good sense to decide what work to do first instead of servicing whoever screams the loudest!!

Parkinson's Law - work expands to fill the time available for its completion

This is true and fits hand in hand with the 80% rule. I am continuously amazed at what I can accomplish when I only allow a limited amount of time. I run my web design business from 5 am to 6 am every morning with an hour or two throughout the week when big projects come up. When I get rained out, and I have all day to sit in front of the computer and work, I tend to not get MUCH more done than when I have the 1-2 hours in the morning!

Ask and receive and take action

I am a true believer that God answers ALL our prayers. Ask for what you need. And then pay attention. Make a decision and ask for guidance. God's guidance is sort of like a car. Turning the steering wheel (asking for guidance) doesn't have much effect unless you're rolling forward. Take a step outside of your comfort zone, make a move, and keep your ears and eyes open.

Watch your language!

Your beliefs dictate your reality, not the other way around. Be impeccable with your language - I know one compadre in the business who has the same equipment he had ten years ago (much of which I sold him VERY used). When I ask him about it, he says, "I HAVE to keep it, I can't AFFORD a new one!! Now I'm sure this is true. But I KNOW that his self talk "keeps" it true. Henry Ford said "whether you think you can do a thing, or think you cannot ... you are right!". I have a relative who recently said "Why bother saving money? every time I do, there's someone waiting to take it". Sure enough, his life situation backs that statement up perfectly, and it's the BELIEF that keeps it that way. Next time you find yourself kicking up this sort of mental manure, change it about. How about "No matter how bad I screw up, I fall ass backwards into money!! It's hilarious!!", "No matter what, I'm going to be successful", "I'm the MAN!!"

Keep walking away costs low

Keep your debt levels in business and in life manageable. Be able to just "up and walk away" if you want. This is my philosophy. It's based on the law of attraction. When you get yourself in a position where you "need" something, you tend to push it away. Such as being in tons of debt and NEEDING a certain amount of work. Also I love the idea of being able to switch gears and do something else with my life if I want. It's a great feeling of freedom.

Integrity

Simply do what you say you're going to do and live by a code, any code, as long as it's yours. Don't let someone else tell you what's right or wrong. If you think it's ok to pay $5 for something and sell it for $50, go ahead! If you don't then don't! Your code is your code. What's right and wrong is probably already pretty ingrained in you, and it "defines" you. Don't compromise it for any reason. It will lessen you in your eyes and the eyes of others. Beware of sayings like "Business is Business". What the hell does that mean?? It's an underlying diseased agreement that says "let's all agree that we have to be moral and upstanding in our personal lives but that we can take the gloves off and use any tactic we need to succeed in business, whether it hurts someone else or not. All's fair in love in war!" When you learn and accept that the only thing to "compete" against is your own limitations and comfort zone, your life will bloom like you can't even imagine.

Golden Rule

Pretty simple: Treat others how you wish to be treated. Be generous, kind, patient, and above all, treat others with respect. If you drop the ball, apologize and make it better, if you blow up at an employee, do the same. Similarly, how you treat others is a reflection of how you treat yourself inside. Chances are, if you are impatient and nasty to someone when they make a mistake, you unconsciously have these feelings toward yourself when you do the same. Everything, everything, everything.

Keep your House Clean!

Look at your life like you would your house. You try to keep it as clean as you can (I hope), but when it gets a little dusty or downright dirty, you clean it up. Do the same with the messes in your life.

Terms

Your "terms" are basically your boundaries, ways of doing business, anything that "defines" you as a person. My terms are basically "this is what I charge, and I deserve it", "you get to dictate the end result, I get to dictate how it's done", "clients stay inside while we're working", "I am paid on time"., "I do what's best for my family", "I live by the golden rule". Terms are not "conditions". There is no "or else" at the end of them. Your terms would be the same, or similar, whether you had a business or not, whether you're single or married with a family of 12. They are simply unspoken bricks that make up who you are as a person and a leader.

Make them GLAD to see you!!

I have clients who pay late. I tend to service them LAST when I'm behind or things aren't running smoothly. Your vendors will do the same with you depending on your payment schedule. When you pay someone late, you're telling them they're not important. Be prepared for them to "tell" you the same with their actions. This one could also go under "Golden Rule". I pay my subs and vendors quickly, and even give my subs a bonus now and again. When I call or need something, they often drop what they're doing just to give us service.

Use screw ups as opportunities!

I have a goal when we make a mistake in our business. Use the opportunity to make the relationship BETTER than it was before the mistake. That might mean replacing a dead plant PLUS giving a free mowing. Or, maybe if we get a complaint call that we didn't get someone plowed out on time, that the plowing is free PLUS we send them a coupon for a free mowing in the spring. You don't have to go overboard, but just go about it as if "these things never happen and we're going to show you how sorry we are".

100% responsibility

Assume that 100% (not 50, 70 or even 90) of your life is your responsibility. Your current life condition in this moment now is a direct manifestation of every thought, word and deed you've had or done up to this moment now. Don't' mistake this for 100% BLAME. Just 100% responsibility. If you can "get to this place" and be there without negativity or "kicking yourself", your life will change. Your power will grow.

One is the loneliest number

My biggest and most effective tip is "don't do it alone". There are those who've gone there before you. Use their wisdom . Read books, make phone calls, take the time and stop and talk with other contractors. Forget that they're your competition.

Diet and Exercise (body)

Yes, you should eat right, drink plenty of water, for heaven's sake don't smoke or drink to excess, easy on the sweets and fat. How you feel physically effects how you feel emotionally and mentally and therefore affects how you PERFORM. Make it a life long habit to stay in shape and have healthy habits. You don't have to be Schwarzenegger. Eat right, stretch and get plenty of water and plenty of rest and sleep. This hasn't changed since the beginning of time.

Diet and Exercise (mind and soul)

Years from now, what I'm about to tell you will be as common sense as the "body" diet advice. Everything you put into your "mind" affects you. Everything. Commercials, violent television, seeing and hearing news about every death in the free world, and on and on. It's very difficult to feel at ease and peace when you allow that garbage into your body. I STRONGLY suggest going on a diet called the "low information" diet. I get my newspaper delivered online and scan the headlines each morning and read whatever catches my fancy. I've only read 2 articles in the past 2 months. I haven't watched the news in TWO YEARS. I do my best to keep a constant stream of reading and other material coming into my "mind and soul" that nourishes my mind, makes me feel good, hopeful, like life is a great mystery worth living. I watch movies that make me feel good or passionate, and wake me up.

These are some thoughts I've written down over the years with the intention of creating a little book for my children, sort of like the "Life's little instruction book" series a few years ago. Read them at least 5 times. Depending on who you are and where you're at, one of them might be the turning point in your life.

"Everything, everything, everything shows up everywhere, everywhere, everywhere."

This is an important axiom to live by. However you show up in one area of your life (shy, impatient, intolerant, generous, etc.) is how you are in every area of your life, although it may "show up" in different ways. Learn to recognize and know "who you are".

You are who you associate with

Always go outside your comfort zone a little with the people you hang with. It's very easy and comfortable to be with those who are a little less educated, intelligent, successful, classy, etc. You will ONLY GROW if you make the majority of your associations a little "higher" than you. Not better, just higher or further along in their development, success, etc.

Be absolute in your intentions.

Decide what you want, period. Don't add "as long as" or "only if" thoughts to what you want. You'll get all the "as long as's" you wish for. Simply decide what you want, face any fears (the "as long as's" and "only ifs") and move toward that.

Focus 90% on your strengths, 10% on your weaknesses or faults

What you focus on grows. Focus on "fixing" or "discovering" what's wrong with you and "what's wrong with you" will grow and grow. Focus on what's great about you and that will grow, leaving the "faults" just kind of sitting there lonely and blue! DO learn about yourself and take time to correct the beliefs you have that don't serve you. Just don't make a career out of it. The universe gives you more of what you focus on.

God helps those who help themselves:

In order to receive God's guidance, we must actually begin the process of action. THEN God will "nudge" us with the many ways that he nudges us! Just like an automobile. The steering wheel doesn't affect the vehicle until it's moving…

Intention / Attraction

If you want something too much, you probably won't get it. "Wanting" something too much is simply affirming that you have a "lack" and you'll simply attract more "lacking and wanting" into your life. Look closely at those who "get" and you'll notice that they did not "want" something, they "desired and decided" to have it.

In business and finance, don't put yourself in a position where you "need" a particular outcome. Murphy's Law (and Law of Attraction) says it probably won't happen!

Someday you will visit a place where all doubt vanishes. When you do, try to stay as long as possible and at least make a commitment to always remember that feeling.

(Hint: it's more of a "lack" of doubt and fear so it feels more like a "lightness" or "freedom" than a sense of power)

You keep what you have by giving it away. You get what you want by giving THAT away also.

(See "the law of giving" from 7 Spiritual Laws of Success and "Conversations with God")

Keep your "walking away "costs in life low. Create your life so that if you want to change jobs, move, finish pursuing your dreams, you can do so without financial ruin. Never be trapped.

What you resist persists. What you "look at" disappears.

"Resisting" grants it energy and holds it even more firmly in place. Looking at it allows you to complete whatever "agenda" you called it for in the first place.

Every circumstance will stay with you until it has completed serving you in all the ways you wanted, needed, chose, and created it to do. The universe sends you that for which you ask. If you refuse your own creation, the universe (as pure Love) assumes you did not hear the message, or missed the sign, and, therefore, sends the gift again — **this time bigger and louder**. Whatever you resist not only persists, but also intensifies.

- (Louix Dor Dempriey)

SELF TRAP! Caution!!
Sometimes when we are uncertain or afraid to commit to something (or get out of something) we subconsciously create a situation where we either trap ourselves in the commitment we're afraid of making or sabotage the situation we're afraid of leaving. This creates lots of pain. Find the courage to change proactively instead of subconsciously.

Decide what your SIMPLE moral code will be and live by it faithfully. "If you don't stand for something, you'll fall for everything".

Always let your children know that they're important, loved, appreciated, wanted, and that what they have to say is valuable.

Eat at least one meal a day as a family

Take care of your parents when they're old and feeble!

Make a list of 10 fears you have in life and get busy tackling them. Don't hurt yourself now!

If someone hurts you, betrays you or violates a boundary, gently but firmly let them know that it's unacceptable and you won't tolerate it again.

Read "Life's Little Instruction Book" series

Watch "It's a wonderful Life"

Watch "Dead Poet's Society"

Watch Andy Griffith and allow yourself to believe that life really can be like Mayberry.

Watch "Heart of Gold" (Neil Young) and allow yourself to be touched

Believe that what you read and watch on TV is JUST as important as what you take into your body.

Always have a "feel good" book that you're in the process of reading and pick "feel good" movies as often as you can stand em'. You'll always be glad afterwards.

Always entertain the possibility that there just might be a Santa Claus. I mean REALLY entertain it!

Don't EVER EVER criticize your children's father (or mother) to them. The ONLY result can be damage to them, damage to the father (or mother) and damage to you. And the damage to the child is ALWAYS the most.

Don't hurry ... Don't wait

If you don't want something to become a habit, don't do it more than 3 times!

Break up big jobs into little tasks.

(A big job is nothing more than a bunch of little ones you didn't do when you should have.)

Practice the spiritual principles of

- Do unto others as you would have them do unto you (Golden Rule)
- Take the next right step and leave the results to God (Intention and Detachment and Right Doing)
- Don't make messes, and when you do ... clean them up right away! (Humility, karma)
- Meditate (Allowing, Detachment)

Do your best to not take things personally

Do your best to be impeccable with your word

- Don't gossip
- Don't criticize yourself

- Don't criticize others
- Don't get laughs at other's expense

QUESTION EVERYTHING, EVERYTHING, EVERYTHING UNTIL YOU'RE SATISFIED YOU'VE GOTTEN THE TRUTH. People tend to be comfortable sheep and deep down, we all love to be "led" and "told what to do". Be a Lion, not a sheep. It's uncomfortable but you'll enjoy the bounty and never look back!

Understand this if nothing else: The journey REALLY IS the most enjoyable part of "getting there", wherever "there" is. Savoring, anticipating and looking forward is really the "appetizer, meal and dessert" of life. The actual destination or event is really just "clearing the table and doing the dishes".

Do something you don't want to do every single day.

Learn a second language … and a third!

Plan a vacation to someplace you might never go.

Climb the steps at St. Paul's Cathedral.

If "everyone's doing it", assume it's probably screwed up!

For You: We bring everything, everything, everything into our lives in some way.

For all of us: We bring everything, everything, everything into our world in some way

The degree to which you resent someone is the degree to which they own you. If someone's gonna rent space in your head, better send them a bill!

Decide what you want, intend it and leave the specific results up to God (law of intention/detachment)

Entertain the thought that there just MIGHT be no such thing as a "tragic, untimely or unfortunate death".

When you catch (a, your) child doing something right that they OFTEN do 'wrong', say "of course they did", not "I can't believe they did, or FINALLY!"

For My Children:

Listen to the mustn'ts, child

Listen to the don'ts

Listen to the shouldn'ts

the impossibles, the won'ts

Listen to the never haves

then listen close to me

Anything can happen, child

Anything can be…

There is no "attention deficit". What you're really seeing is attention ABUNDANCE.

For Fathers of Daughters:

The biggest gift you can give to your daughter is to show her how a great husband loves his wife. Do this for 18 years and she'll find a man who will do it for her for the next 60 or so.

For Husbands

The greatest gifts you can give to your wife are to compliment her in public, let her know as often as you can how lucky you are that she chose you, and always, and I mean always, let her have 100% credit for the success of your marriage.

Additional Bonus Material (new stuff!)

Tips for working efficiently

After writing this book, I began, of course, to pay more attention to the things I'd written about to make sure that I was "practicing what I preach" as well as to glean any more great information that I could pass on to you, faithful reader.

What I've been discovering are many little "under the radar" tips, techniques and "styles" if you will that seem to move the day along quickly and efficiently. Here's a list to start off your day!

When loading a wheelbarrow, your feet shouldn't move!

Put your wheel barrow RIGHT next to your loam, mulch or other material and start shoveling. It should take approx. 2/3 of a second per shovelful. I saw someone loading loam from a trailer into a WB the other day, but they'd placed the WB next to the trailer, so each shovelful meant he had to turn around, walk 2 steps and deposit the shovel into the WB. This operation took about 6 seconds per shovel!!!

Park your truck next to your work

This is one of the most common violated, but most time saving technique you can use. Park your truck near the bulk of your work, and don't be afraid to stop, take a break and move it if that location changes. That way when you need a new tool, have to load debris, etc. it's right there. The difference between doing this consciously or NOT can mean the difference, on average, of a mile walking and a half hour extra time. That's substantial! It's all about being conscious.

Work fairly steady and fast, take more breaks (optional)

I've found that working steady and fast and taking breaks when needed gets me further along than "slow and steady" all day. Of course I only work 4-5 hours a day so this might be more of a challenge if you're the dusk till dawn type. I've just found that you focus more this way and for some reason, you just get more done hustling for 45 and breaking for 15 than an hour of plodding along.

Clean your messes at the end, NOT as you go

Other than making sure you're not tripping over materials or leaving anything dangerous around, clean up at the end, not as you go. I'm referring to actual work areas, where you know you're going to have to clean the SAME thing up again at the end anyway. That's the key here. Don't cleanup something that you're going to have to cleanup again at the end. Do things once.

Avoid left hand turns if you live in a busy area

This one tip can save you a hundred hours of drive time, especially on a multi stop mowing route. When you take a right turn, you've turning with traffic and have the right of way. Left turns almost always take longer because you're turning against on coming traffic, often from the right and straight ahead. I know a company in Las Vegas that actually has a computer generated route that minimizes or eliminates all left hand turns against traffic on their mowing routes.

Keep Everything in the Truck

Keep every tool you'll need for your "usual" line of work in your truck. During hedge trimming time, keep all your ladders, trimmers, etc. in your truck. During mowing take everything for that. This eliminates one step of "thinking" each morning and eliminates those money eating return trips to the shop.

Leave Neutral Messages

It's tempting when you discover "sloppy work" or some other problem to call the person responsible and leave a heated message. Remember that you don't know the story yet. Leave a neutral "call me as soon as possible" message and then give thought to what you're going to say.

Resources (Also Known as "Important Stuff")

Here are some books and other resources that will either alone, or in combination, change your life and way of being for the better. These SHOULD be all you need to answer any question you might have about the lawn and landscape business, the nature of money or even your own purpose in life!

Lawn Care and Landscape Specific Books and Web Resources:

- http://www.martygrunder.com/home.html - Marty Grunder's Winners' Circle. Do this boot camp. Do it now.

- Clip forum, lawn-talk - signup for Lawn Talk at www.LawnGuru.net

- lawnsite.com - The Original And Largest Online Community In The Green Industry!

- lawncafe.com - Same nature as lawnsite

- scotts.com - Great info on pests, lawn science and advice on fertilizers and pest control

- pestweb.com - Leading pest control resource

- weedalert.com - The Turf Professional's Online Source for Weed Control Options.

- thinkfirstspraylast.org - Maine Board of Pesticides

Control - many resources including posting signs, requirements, links to other pest related resources nationwide.

- http://www.maine.gov/agriculture/pesticides/cert/calibrate.htm - calibrating your spraying or pesticide equipment

- http://www.rndsigns.com/ - site signs, door hangers, and pesticide recertification online classes. I've used these, they're simple and great.

- www.lesco.com - great supplier of pesticides and pesticide related products.

- www.nutrientsplus.com - very reasonably priced, effective organic and organic BASED fertilizers and lawn treatments. I've used them, they're great.

- www.dutchbulbs.com - where I get ALL my lily bulbs

- www.colorblends.com - where I get ALL my tulip bulbs

- Landscaperpro.com - landscape equipment and parts, some as much as 50% off dealer price.

- Drafix Software (Pro Landscape Design Software)

- http://www2.hometime.com/Admin/shopsite/v_land.htm - How-to videos of various landscape projects

Other Business Books and Web Resources

- Intuit.com (QuickBooks Pro)

- Prosper.com - website dedicated to connecting lenders and borrowers. Yes, you can literally borrow $20,000 from someone you don't know in Walla Walla Washington!

- http://www.onepagebusinessplan.com/

- Pro Magazine (Cygnus publications) - great magazine that profiles different lawn care companies throughout North America

Spiritual, Personal Development and Business Books and Web Resources:

- StevePavlina.com - The single best resource I've ever found for personal and spiritual development

- http://www.fourhourworkweek.com/ - The Four Hour Work Week by Tim Ferris

- The eMyth Revisited (contractor version) - **contractor or regular version available**

- **Links to all these books and videos can be found at** http://lawnguru.net/personal-spiritual-development-books.shtml

- The Four Agreements - Don Miguel Ruiz

- Way of the peaceful Warrior - Dan Millman

- Ask and it is Given - Abraham-Hicks Publications

- Conversations with God series by Neale Donald Walsh

- The Power of Now - Eckhart Tolle

- Radical Forgiveness - Colin Tipping

- Type Z Guide To Success - Marc Allen (all his work is worth reading)

- Think and Grow Rich - Napoleon Hill - The 'Father' of the Law of Attraction

- The Secret - Great video on the law of attraction. A Must Have.

- The Sterling Men's Weekend. www.higherpurpose.com - Personally changed my life and helped me become a better father, husband, leader and entrepreneur.

SAMPLE CLIENT SURVEY

Your Name _____   E mail Address_____

PLEASE list your email address if I don't already have it so I can communicate

with you more effectively. Your address will, of course, remain private. I often send alerts and reminders to my clients via email to save time and deliver better service and communication. We will also be switching to email billing starting August first unless you tell us otherwise. Thanks so much!

Month and Day of birth(optional)_____(so we can say "happy birthday")

We are absolutely determined to deliver such great service you wouldn't dream of being without us. In order to make that happen **we need your help**. Our best source of information is you. How are we doing? What can we do different? Where are we "dropping the ball? What are we doing that makes you smile so we can do MORE of that?" These are valuable questions that really only you can answer. So you're not just our client, you are our partner in many ways. To show you how valuable I believe your input is, I'll be taking $5.00 off your bill when you send this completed form back! **If you get this survey with your bill, take $5 off that bill**. Thanks for having us, and with your help, we'll only get better and better.

Key: 1) poor   2) fair   3) good   4)very good   5)excellent!

Using the key above, rate us on a scale of 1-5 on the following items:

1. quality of work: ___
   comments_____

2. timeliness of work: ___
   comments_____

3. Integrity: ___ (did we do what we said we were going to do and if we erred we took care of it)

4. Communication: ___
   comments_____

5. Clarity of billing: ___
   comments:_____

6. Value of work vs. price: ___ (did you get your money's worth)

7. Politeness and professionalism of crew: ___
   comments_____

8. Appearance of crew/equipment: ___
   comments_____

9. How well do you feel "taken care of": ___
   comments:_____

10. Knowledge of owner and crew: ___
    comments_____

11. Other comments _____

    _____

11. All things considered, would you say our service is better, worse or the same as last year?_____

12. Have you recommended us to your friends and/or neighbors?   Yes   No

If yes, thank you, if no, please do OR send me their name and number and I'd be happy to tactfully

Contact them. All clients receive $10 off their next bill with each successful referral.

Notes:

Printed in the United States
138919LV00003BA/90/P